The Hero of Our Story

A commentary on Ramana Maharshi's
"Vision of Reality"

The Hero of Our Story

A commentary on Ramana Maharshi's "Vision of Reality"

Edwin Faust

MANTRA
BOOKS

Winchester, UK
Washington, USA

JOHN HUNT PUBLISHING

First published by Mantra Books, 2022
Mantra Books is an imprint of John Hunt Publishing Ltd., No. 3 East Street, Alresford
Hampshire SO24 9EE, UK
office@jhpbooks.com
www.johnhuntpublishing.com
www.mantra-books.net

For distributor details and how to order please visit the 'Ordering' section on our website.

ISBN: 978 1 78535 937 8
978 1 78535 938 5 (ebook)
Library of Congress Control Number: 2021949204

A CIP catalogue record for this book is available from the British Library.

Design: Matthew Greenfield

UK: Printed and bound by CPI Group (UK) Ltd, Croydon, CR0 4YY
Printed in North America by CPI GPS partners

We operate a distinctive and ethical publishing philosophy in all areas of our business, from our global network of authors to production and worldwide distribution.

Genuine "knowledge" of God is commonly thought of as being restricted to saints, sages, advanced yogis or ancient mystics. Among such luminaries, Ramana Maharshi has become perhaps the most revered among contemporary seekers drawn to *Advaita*, the non-dual "understanding" that literally all things are the Lord. Unfortunately, even ardent devotees of Ramana rarely experience fruition of their search, lost in the subtleties and concepts of non-dual texts, teachers, and even the teachings of Ramana himself. Thankfully, Edwin Faust's commentary on Ramana's *Sat-Darshanam,* provides a penetrating vision through the fog of delusion and spiritual fantasy to the heart of the fullness and perfection of the One. For those sensing frustrations with meditation, yoga, prayer, and other forms of striving for inner freedom, Faust's text sounds like a fresh breeze, gently sweeping away layers of conditioning and misguided concepts, allowing us finally to "see" what has always been there.

Dr. Robert Sitler
Professor of World Languages and Cultures
Stetson University

Introduction

Whether I shall turn out to be the hero of my own life, or whether that station will be held by anybody else, these pages must show.
David Copperfield by Charles Dickens

The other day I watched a child set down on the beach by her father. She was about two years old and immediately took off, with all the speed with which her little legs could carry her, toward a group of seagulls. The gulls, old hands at this business, bided their time, flying off a second before she reached them. The little girl chased the birds this way and that, and her course brought her closer and closer to the water's edge. When the last few gulls flew away, she stopped in her tracks, suddenly aware of the ocean. She stared, frozen with uncertainty, then raised her arms, as though she were about to walk a tightrope, and took a few tentative steps into the foam of the receding waves. She decided she liked the feel of the water on her feet and began to stomp and spin and squeal with delight. It did my heart good to watch this happy little scene, and I thought that it might stand as a tableau for life's chase.

Most of us run after this and that – wealth, pleasure, reputation – but we never really catch the gull; that is, we never reach a place where we can stop and say, "Yes. Now I have arrived. This is where I wanted to be and where I will remain. This is happiness." Our running can continue until we run out of breath, out of life. But some of us are fortunate enough to find ourselves at the water's edge, so to speak, where we notice the ocean for the first time. Its splendor, its ceaseless rhythm, is arresting. We stand and stare and feel that somewhere in the distance and the depths lies the answer to the mystery of who we are.

These mystical moments happen to all of us: moments

in which we sense that life offers us something rich and wonderful; something beyond the banality of running after what the world calls success. We then begin to recognize that our list of accomplishments has little to do with who we really are and what we really want. We begin to ask in earnest "Who am I?" Finding the answer to this question can acquire a sense of urgency. When it comes to overshadow all other concerns, we will have arrived at the threshold of self-knowledge. But the steps we take beyond that threshold do not always move us in a straight line toward what we seek.

A burning desire to know who we are does not, in itself, remove our conditioning. We tend to approach Self-inquiry in the same way we have approached life: as a quest for success through action. We still hope to redeem ourselves through some singular achievement or experience. We merely shift the arena from the outer world to the inner world. And we look for a hero to emulate; someone whose path to greatness we can retrace. This may partly explain why Ramana Maharshi has become a figure of romance for many Western seekers. His story appeals to our idea of the hero and the quest. He is seen as the Great Soul we want to become.

His biography fascinates us: a young man galvanized by a dramatic revelation leaves home abruptly, travels a great distance to a holy place, seeks out solitude in subterranean temple chambers and remote caves, immerses himself in prolonged states of deep meditation, experiences ecstatic states of consciousness; an ashram is built, as it were, around him, at the base of the sacred mount of Arunachala, and world-weary seekers travel from the far corners of the Earth to sit at the feet of the saint, eager for a look or a word that will transform their lives. Testimonials accumulate. Even after the saint is gone, the place where he dwelt becomes a place of international pilgrimage. To this day, many Westerners come to circumambulate the sacred mount, perhaps dreaming of becoming another Ramana; of finding their own cave and plunging so deeply into meditation that they will never leave it, living always in ecstasy, with the world passing before them like a play of shadows, unable to touch them further with its illusory problems and pains.

This is the dream Ramana, a fantasy about who he was and who we might become. But there is the real Ramana, and he was only concerned with who we are, for there is nothing we can become. The real Ramana is to be found in his writing. And in his chief work, *Sat-Darshanam*, we meet, not the ethereal holy man of spiritual romance whose feet barely touched the ground, but the solid vision of Vedanta as given to us in the Upanishads and unfolded in the teaching tradition from time immemorial.

There is an errant notion that Ramana is outside this tradition; that he discovered the truths proclaimed in the Upanishads independently of them. And if he did it, perhaps we can do it, too. And some of us hope to duplicate the supposedly revelatory experience we believe Ramana must have had at some definitive moment of enlightenment. This imagined moment is generally assumed to have occurred for Ramana while he was deep in the yogic trance called *samadhi*.

There is much we don't know about Ramana, but we know this: whatever he experienced in *samadhi* was just that – an experience. And there is a difference between having an experience and having knowledge. *Samadhi*, deep sleep, even psychedelic drugs can deliver an experience of non-duality: we feel the bliss of oneness, of there no longer being a painful and anxious division between us and the world and God. But no one wakes up in the morning enlightened as a result of deep sleep, nor does one come down from an LSD trip as a liberated being. And *samadhi* also is an event that occurs in time: it has a beginning and an end, which means it is not real, as Vedanta defines reality.

Meditation is an action, not a means of knowledge, a *pramana*. It can help calm and purify the mind, loosening the hold of desires. It can deliver states of bliss. But bliss will come and go. It will not deliver knowledge. And it is through knowledge alone that we can free ourselves from ignorance and its attendant miseries. Vedanta alone leads to non-dual knowledge.

Ramana, however, was not a typical student of Vedanta, for he had no doubts to resolve, nor did he require long periods of contemplation to became established in the truth. Ramana's years of meditation had removed the obstacles to knowledge most of us encounter. These obstacles are attachments to the world, desires that still bind us. They muddy the mind. But Ramana's mind was so lucid that he needed only to hear the truth of the Self to realize it fully and immediately. The pundits read him the scriptures and he saw the vision of the Upanishads, the *Sat-Darshanam*. And that was that. He stopped going into *samadhi*. He left the experience of non-duality to live in the knowledge of non-duality.

Ramana was that rarest of beings, what Vedanta calls *uttama adhikari* – highly qualified. Most of us are located rather lower in the scale of aspirants. We hear the truth and we see the light, then the darkness closes in again. We have to make our way back to the light with effort and determination. We have to pursue a Vedantic sadhana, which involves listening to the teaching repeatedly, examining our doubts, spending time in contemplation. And we need a traditional teacher.

Ramana was not a traditional teacher. He spent a great deal of time sitting in silence, surrounded by adoring devotees who believed that mere physical proximity to him would somehow liberate them from their problems. One even encounters the claim, supposedly endorsed by Ramana's example, "Silence is the best teacher." Someone once asked the great Vedantin Swami Dayananda, if this were true. He smiled and said, "If it were true, all the pages of the Upanishads would be blank."

Ramana's verses may not be readily comprehended by Vedanta students who are fairly new to self-inquiry. His teaching is advanced and his verses, greatly compressed. While Vedanta has several teaching methods it uses to investigate the nature of the individual, the world and God, Ramana focuses on inquiry into the nature of the individual. He has an Occam's Razor approach: he cuts away everything except the question, "Who am I?" When this is answered, he maintains, all else is answered.

Some books have been published which are arranged collections of answers Ramana gave to individuals who questioned him about aspects of sadhana and Self-inquiry in a group setting called *satsang*. They are part of the growing mass of *satsang* literature which, despite its value, can never be a substitute for a systematic unfoldment of the texts of Vedanta. Indeed, this literature can lead to confusion, as the answers provided are terse, often specific to an individual circumstance, and in need of further explanation, which they seldom receive. The reader can go from one question to another, eating the answers like popcorn, until he is full, but he will obtain little genuine nourishment in the end. With few exceptions, the hunger for self-knowledge can only be satisfied by the tried-and-true methods of Vedanta. And a competent teacher rooted in the tradition is indispensable. No *satsang* book or romantic dream can take the teacher's place.

Ramana's lasting contribution to the science of self-inquiry can be found in his written work, but that work must be unfolded in the same manner as any other text that deals with self-inquiry. I am not a teacher of Vedanta, but I do find it helpful to write about whatever understanding I have received from those who are good teachers. It is a way to practice *nididhyasana* – the contemplation of the truth.

This contemplation is necessary for most of us, for hearing the truth does not free us immediately from the ignorance that has kept us bound for countless lifetimes. This is not to say that *moksha* – liberation – depends upon contemplation, which is not a means of knowledge. It merely helps us to arrive at a mental clarity that allows the truth to be always available to us. It is not the case that contemplation gives us anything so much as it takes away the habitual thoughts inimical to seeing the vision of Vedanta. And this vision comes only by listening to the teaching – *sravana*. Westerners have been conditioned to think of the spiritual life as an exercise of the will to bring action into conformity with virtue. We have an almost unconscious assumption that salvation or *moksha* (liberation) is necessarily a matter of morals and muscle. This is why yoga has such a strong appeal in Europe and the Americas: it gives us something to do, along with prescribing rules for diet and conduct – a program we can put into action. But as long as we believe action will lead us to liberation, Vedanta will be either unintelligible to us or, more likely, misunderstood. It is rather good news that liberation can be had by listening, but it seems too good to be true. And there are many teachers who will tell us that the texts of Vedanta are subject to verification by experience. In other words, experience becomes the ultimate *pramana*, the true means of knowledge. This is not Vedanta, and it is not what Ramana taught.

What follows is an attempt to make Ramana's expression of the vision of Vedanta more accessible to people who may have a keen interest in Ramana but remain perplexed, or even misled, about what is involved in asking the question, "Who am I?"

The following English text of *Sat-Darshanam* is A.R. Natarajan's translation of the Sanskrit text of Ganapati Muni, which is a translation of the original text which Ramana wrote in Tamil. So, we are looking at a translation of a translation. This English text, with facing Sanskrit, is published by the Ramana Maharshi Center for Learning and has been accepted as reliable by those entrusted with Ramana's legacy. It should also be noted that other English translations exist, which do not contradict and often enrich the principal English text presented below.

Sat-Darshanam

Prayer

Can there be the feeling of "I" without that which exists always!
Free from thoughts, it exists, this inner being, the heart.
How then to know that which is beyond the mind?
To know it is to abide firmly, in the heart.

Ramana begins this work in the traditional manner, with verses of benediction. These preliminary words usually acknowledge the writer's indebtedness to the teacher or are offered in praise of his chosen deity. Ramana, however, devotes his opening lines to the truth he is about to expound. He gives a summation of that truth which, if properly understood, would obviate the need to read further. For the highly qualified student, the text could end here.

The opening verse begins by posing a question, which might be paraphrased as "Can that 'I' which comes and goes be experienced by me unless there is an 'I' which does not come and go?" The "I" feeling referred to here is that identification of the Self with our experience; and as our experience is always changing, the "I" feeling is likewise always changing.

How many different experiences of "I" feeling do we have in the course of a day? At 11 a.m. we may think, "I am smart," and by noon we may think, with equal conviction, "I am stupid." Both opinions are triggered by something that has happened or by some memory that has recurred. Which opinion is true? Neither. For that which is real does not come and go: it remains in past, present and future. This is the definition of reality (*vastu*).

Reality, in Vedantic parlance, is that which cannot be negated. Negation (*badhita*) occurs when one thought-form is replaced by another. Every thought about the body and mind

7

can be negated. In fact, it inevitably will be negated. Try to stop this from happening and see how well you succeed.

Change is all we seem to experience despite an intense and often painful longing for that which does not change. Yet, who is the knower of change? Can change be known except by that which does not change? Is not the "I" that witnesses the I-am-stupid thought the same "I" that witnesses the I-am-smart thought? Is there not an "I" that is real, that is unaffected by the ceaseless flux of thoughts, the never-ending process of negation?

This is the principal question asked by one who has begun seriously to wonder who he really is. And this is where Ramana starts his *Sat-Darshanam*: the changing "I" depends upon the unchanging "I."

So what is this unchanging "I"?

We begin each "I" thought with "I am_____," then we fill in the blank variously. If the blanks we fill in, the attributes we assume to be our nature, can be negated, they cannot be the real "I." As these "I" thoughts dissolve, one after another, to be replaced by the succeeding thought, the one thing that is ever present is the "I am." We, as conscious beings, persist amid all the changing experiences. In fact, without the constant "I am," the chameleon "I am such and such" – the ego – cannot exist. In fact, it does not exist in the strict sense, but appears as a series of fleeting and intermittent thoughts to the changeless aware being that we always are.

In Shankaracharya's *Laghu Vakya Vritti*, we are told, "Pure consciousness should be distinguished from reflected consciousness with great effort (*atiyatnaha*)." What is "pure consciousness?" Ramana identifies it as the "Heart," that is, our core identity. Reflected consciousness is the "I" feeling – the shifting thoughts that we superimpose upon the genuine "I," which is "free from thoughts." This distinction is not easily made, which is why Shankara adds the phrase, "with great effort" and why Ramana writes 39 more verses.

Some translations opt for "devoid of thoughts" instead of "free from thoughts," but the latter seems the better wording as it is less liable to cause misunderstanding. There are teachers and explanatory texts that advocate the unqualified destruction of the mind, whatever that may mean. Such counsel is often attributed to Ramana. But the mind is given us as an instrument of knowledge. Without our ability to reason, to discriminate, there would be little point to a teaching that offers us freedom from the tyranny of identifying with experience. In fact, if the destruction of the mind were the *summum bonum*, lobotomies would be a direct path to liberation and teachers could be replaced by brain surgeons.

Without going too far afield at this early stage, it might be worth mentioning that human beings in the waking state cannot be "devoid of thoughts." We can, however, be "free from thoughts." This means we do not identify with the thoughts that come and go and that constitute what we call experience. The thought, "I am stupid" may occur to someone who is enlightened as well as to someone still struggling with ignorance, but their respective reactions will differ: one who has self-knowledge will not be affected by the thought; one who does not will believe that his "I" is indeed a stupid "I" and will experience all the embarrassment, regret and humiliation that identifying with such a thought visits upon him.

These revolving "I" thoughts bring us pleasure and pain, but mostly pain. We try to maximize the one and minimize the other, but the wheel keeps turning and we cannot stop it. The good news is that we are not our shifting thoughts. If we were, we would have no stable sense of the Self. Yet we do have such a sense. It is the one thing we can never lose. We can think we are many different things, but we cannot think ourselves out of existence. Try it and see what happens.

The philosopher David Hume thought he had succeeded

in analyzing the Self out of existence. He reasoned that he is always conscious of something, and that "something" is forever changing. He concluded that belief in a stable Self is simply that – a belief; and he could find no empirical evidence to justify such a belief. Hume identified the Self as a "bundle of perceptions," some of which recur in memory, lending us a false sense of stability. The idea that there exists an unchanging "I" was, in Hume's view, a mere habit. He was, in some ways, aligned with certain Buddhist notions.

What Hume failed to consider properly is the nature of consciousness itself. He thought that consciousness must inhere in an object, and as objects appear one after another, without stopping, consciousness can be no more than an ever-moving kaleidoscope of perceptions. But when one object succeeds another, who is it that notices the change? Does consciousness cease to exist in between perceptions? And there must be an "in between" or else there could be no change, no progression in which one perception ends and another begins. If there were no "pure" or constant consciousness, change could not be perceived at all: we could not say, "I thought this and now I think that."

To call the "I" sense, our core identity, a habit does not explain why it persists. And it is strangely ironic that so brilliant a thinker as Hume does not take into account the fact that he is trying to establish a truth, that is, an unchanging declaration about the nature of consciousness. Had he pondered a little more deeply, with greater courage and determination, he might have reached a more profound understanding. But as he cavalierly admits, when the perplexity of these questions pressed in upon him with too much urgency, he would take a glass of wine and play a game of backgammon. In short, Hume lacked the crucial qualification for inquiry into the nature of the Self: *mumukshutvam* – an intense desire for liberation, for the truth.

Ramana was on fire with this desire, which led him to leave home at the age of 16 and devote himself entirely to the pursuit of knowledge about his self-identity. In this first line of his prayer verses, Ramana gives us the entire fruit of his quest; in fact, he gives us the essence of Vedanta.

Anyone who tries to write about Vedanta soon comes to know the difficulty of doing so, which resides in the fact that the truth about who we are is both simple and profound: it can be expressed in a few words, but those few words can give rise to libraries of commentaries that try to reach the depth of understanding they contain. And words express the apparent differences in a world of objects, not the non-dual ground of all being; so, they must be handled very carefully and used to indicate that which they cannot contain or define.

The first word in the prayer verse is *satpratyayah*. In the text we are using, it is translated as "the feeling of I." This is not a literal or exclusive meaning. Swami Paramarthananda translates it, as do others, as "experience," which he defines as **existence plus an object**.

Swami Paramarthananda says that in every experience two things are involved: existence, which he calls the "E-principle," and an object. We do not see existence, however; we see the object, to which we attribute existence. But objects have no existence in themselves. If they did, they could not come and go: they would always be. What is real, what persists through all changes, is existence, what Ramana calls *santam* in the first line of the verse.

We are being asked at the outset to realize the distinction between existence and objects – the real "I" and the "I" feeling which identifies with changing perceptions. And we are being asked to recognize that without existence, objects could not be perceived, for they would not be. This existence, this E-principle on which all objects depend, including our shifting "I" feeling, is our true identity, our true "I," which Ramana calls the "Heart."

But as this true "I" – our Heart – cannot be perceived in our changing thoughts, how are we to know it? In fact, we cannot know it in the way we know objects, which exist in time. We can only know our heart by abiding in our heart. The Self cannot be externalized and perceived, for then it would join the ranks of those things which come and go and we would still be faced with the question: "What is aware of the things that come and go but itself does not come and go?"

So how do we abide in the Heart, that is, in the changeless core of our being, our true Self? This is the question Ramana will address in the succeeding verses.

The "I" thought is the first to die for those who have taken refuge, out of fear
Of death, at the feet of the conqueror of death!
Thereafter, they are naturally immortal.
Can they ever again be assailed by the fear of death?

Fear of death is held by some to be the ground of all religion, for what we seek from God is an assurance that we will not ultimately cease to exist with the death of the body. But if we think we are the body, as most of us do, it is difficult to believe that we can continue to live without it.

When we ask, "Who am I?" are we not asking, "Will I die when the body dies? Am I really no more than flesh and blood, than a torrent of thoughts and fleeting sensations? Is there anything about me that is real, that lasts?"

Recall that Swami Parmarthananda defined perception as existence plus an object. We make a mistake when we attribute existence to the object, as though it were self-sufficient, rather than dependent. But having made the mistake, we then fear that the objects we love will disappear, as they surely will; chief among these is the body. It is this fear that drives people to a God they hope will save them from disappearing when the body dies.

Christian sects generally require belief in what they call "the resurrection of the body." Christ, it is dogmatically declared, rose from the dead with his body intact, and so eventually will those of his followers who have satisfied certain requirements. Most Christians hope to please God sufficiently to be admitted into His domain, where death is no more and where, in some fashion, they can retain their accustomed identities along with new and improved bodies at the end of time.

Other religions maintain various conceptions of the afterlife, but no religion offers a means of knowledge for establishing the certain or exclusive truth of its claims. So, can any of these deities that are worshiped with the hope of attaining what is called "salvation," i.e., a happy life after death, be the "conqueror of death" Ramana refers to in the above verse?

This conqueror delivers what the other gods are supposed to have in their gift – immortality – but it does so, not by preserving the limited identity and providing it with a new body, but by killing it. In fact, we are told that the "I" thought is the first thing to go when one seeks refuge in the conqueror of death, and the fruit of this annihilation is an end to the fear of death. Why is the death of the "I" thought given priority as the requisite for immortality?

The "I" thought that must die here is not the true "I" – the heart – mentioned in the previous verse; it is rather the "I" feeling: the changing perceptions to which we mistakenly attribute existence, especially our individual existence. Because these perceptions all come and go, that is, they are all born and they all die, so long as we identify with them, we cannot escape the fear of death.

Now, God, however we conceive of such a being, is necessarily a thought: it is existence – the "E-principle" – plus God, the object. No matter how exalted our notion of God, and no matter how sublime a mystical experience we may have of this God, we cannot confer existence upon a thought, nor can a thought return the favor: I worship you, and in return, you give my "I" feeling immortality.

So, by the "conqueror of death" Ramana cannot mean the conventional notion of God, or any notion at all. He can only mean the heart, as described in the first verse. And when one abides in this heart, one is "free from thoughts," including all thoughts of a deity. This heart, let's recall, is existence itself (*santam*), our true "I." This is why Ramana says that when the "I" thought dies, we are "naturally immortal."

If we are "naturally immortal," then this immortality cannot be the result of any action, of any worship or supplication to a deity. It does not come into being when the "I" thoughts die; it is rather that when we are free of the "I" thoughts we realize who we always were and can never cease to be. That which is natural is not that which we acquire; it is that which we cannot be without. It is who we are.

The epithet "conqueror of death" is a name for *Shiva*. And *Shiva*, in turn, is a name for *Ishwara*. And *Ishwara* is the infinite creative knowledge of *Brahman*. And *Brahman* is *Atma*. And *Atma* is me. I am the conqueror of death! Ramana is saying that once we know who we are, we can never again be subject to the fear of death, which is rooted in notions of who we are not.

But these notions, these "I" thoughts, have been with us for a very long time and are reluctant to depart. To abide in the heart requires more than a flash of insight. Ramana knows this and so he proceeds to help us develop the necessary discrimination in the verses that follow.

Verse 1

Because we see the variegated world, a single source,
With unlimited powers, has to be accepted.
The seer, the seen, the screen on which it is projected, the light,
Are all only He, the One.

Following the prayer verses, Ramana begins *Sat-Darshanam* with a grand overview of our basic situation as individuals in a world of objects. We are here; the world is out there. Neither we nor the world are self-sufficient. We then conclude there must be something else – a third thing – that has brought us and the world into being. This third thing is what the text calls a "single source, with unlimited powers."

Why a "single source"? Because if there are many sources, many gods, then there must be some limitation to each god's power that distinguishes it from the rest. A god – or source of power – that is limited, can offer only a partial explanation of a particular domain; that limited god also requires a cause: a superior that assigns limitations to this collection of subordinate causes, of which he is but one among many. Without a single source of unlimited power, we would be left with an infinite regress.

An argument for a single source of the manifest world also appears in the West as the Uncaused Cause, found in the scholastic tradition and traceable to Aristotle. It says that everything we perceive is dependent upon a cause outside of itself: I am caused by my parents, who in turn were caused by theirs, who in turn, etc. But this regression of causes must come to an end. It must come to rest in that which in itself is uncaused and which sets all other causes in motion. This is what most people call God, or "a single source, with unlimited power."

In Gaudapada's *Karika*, a famous text of Vedanta, the author says that all religions, even the most insistently dualistic, posit non-duality as the source or ground of all that is perceived to exist. God is always spoken of as being infinite, timeless, changeless, perfect and indivisible. Gaudapada sees no point in disputing with the proponents of any particular religion, but proceeds directly to an examination of the non-duality they all acknowledge.

There is general agreement among those who have thought about the nature of dependent being that a single source, with unlimited power, is needed. I exist, the world exists, and one power makes both of us manifest. How are we to conceive of such a power?

Ramana offers us a picture, literally. He presents us with the image of a painted canvas. The painting depicts all manner of objects, inert and sentient. But all the objects appear on one canvas from which they are indivisible. The seeming diversity is, in fact, one substance appearing as though it were many things. We can also take the metaphor as that of a motion picture: all the images appear on the same screen, made visible by the same light; that is, made known by one consciousness, from which they are inseparable.

If there is a single source, with unlimited power that accounts for everything, what are we to make of the seeming diversity of objects? Ramana begins to address this in the following verse.

Verse 2

All religions begin with the existence of the individual,
The world and God.
So long as the ego lasts, these three will remain separate.
To abide, egoless, in the Self, is the best.

When we awake in the morning, we are aware of our body, then of the objects in the room and in the wider world. If we are religious, we may also think of the God whom we acknowledge as our Creator, and begin the day with a prayer.

Deities of varied forms are given their daily tribute. Even the materialist, although his first thought may be of his breakfast, has his belief in the omnipotence called Evolution, which is as mysterious and inexorable a force as the Calvinist God of Predestination.

Ramana tells us that all religions deal with three things: the individual, the world in which he lives, and the God who is responsible for both. But religions disagree, often sharply, in their assessment of human nature and how men should relate to one another. They also have divergent views on the deity, the sort of worship he requires and the code of conduct he prescribes. And the afterlife, if included in a particular creed, can take different shapes.

To engage in polemics about which religion is correct is not only pointless but potentially dangerous. It is pointless because no independent means of knowledge is available within a particular creed to establish its truth or falsity. An appeal to a record of supposed Revelation does not resolve the difficulty, as it involves circular reasoning: we trust in a book because it's God's word, and we know it is God's word because the book says so. And contending scriptures present an often radically different version of what is claimed to be absolute

17

truth, as do contending interpretations of the same scripture. The consequent polemics are dangerous as they tend to end in a vilification of those who hold opposing beliefs, and there are "scriptures" that enjoin holy war against infidels. People are seldom more merciless than when they are killing others in the name of God.

Ramana begins this verse by stating a general fact: we find ourselves to be individuals in a universe that arose from a source outside of us, and that source is generally called God.

Ramana looks directly at how this three-fold division comes about. He says it has its root and sustenance in the ego; that is, the "I" thought. And he tells us that this division will last so long as we identify the Self with the body and the mind and their varying conditions.

The best thing, the highest thing (*sarvottama*) is to stop thinking we are the changing "I" thought and remain in the true I – the heart mentioned in the opening prayer verse. In that heart, we remain free of all the changing circumstances that we confuse with our Self and that constitute what is here called the ego. When we remain in the heart, in the core of our being, the three-fold division will disappear, along with all of its attendant problems.

Does this mean the world will dissolve, along with its God, when the ego is negated? If so, what will remain? Quite simply, I will remain. The world and God, as separate from me, depend on my thinking that I am separate from them. When I realize that all of my notions appear in the consciousness that is me, and that this consciousness cannot be divided, then all sense of separation ends. Recall the metaphor of the painted canvas.

Some who seek the truth favor an inquiry into the nature of the world, or the nature of God. Ramana maintains that if we inquire into the nature of the "I" and come to reside in the heart, all difficulties about the world and God will be taken care of.

Verse 3

Of what use are disputes such as "the world is real,"
"No, it is a mirage," "it is conscious energy,"
"No, it is matter," "it is happiness," "no, it is sorrow."
Abidance in the exalted state where neither the ego nor the world exists
Is acceptable to all.

When we first discover philosophy, we may be thrilled by the prospect of exploring the ultimate questions with the tools of logic. There arises the hope that certain knowledge, a provable and indisputable truth, is discoverable if only we apply ourselves diligently to our inquiry. But as we proceed in our study, that hope begins to fade.

We find that every idea, no matter how promising it may appear, is soon challenged by another idea that negates or modifies it. And that idea in its turn suffers the same fate. Each road of inquiry branches into several more roads and, no matter which one we follow, that path also diverges and we wander farther and farther into a tangled terrain that stretches toward an ever-receding horizon.

Once we begin to search for the causes of objects, which is what constitutes inquiry into the world, our senses no longer serve as a means of knowledge. David Hume was right to say that we do not perceive causes when we observe objects interacting, such as one billiard ball striking another; we see sequences and infer causes. And our inferences are subject to modification as we learn more about objects and their properties. This is why there is no such thing as "settled science." No object has a fixed content, a form that cannot be further reduced.

And if we cannot definitively identify cause and effect in the world of objects, what chance have we of doing so when it comes to the cosmos? The universe is really but the total collection of objects that we perceive, so the same difficulties we face in understanding the microcosm apply to the macrocosm.

And the search for truth about the nature and cause of the world is further complicated by the human ego, which inserts itself into the inquiry. Once we adopt a position, it becomes "my position." The "I" thought is now identified with an idea, and any challenge to that idea is a threat to me. I am then no longer purely interested in the truth, but in defending an idea I take to be mine. Debate then becomes a pointless exercise in self-assertion or self-defense. It will not lead to a resolution of the question at hand.

Ramana says that such fruitless speculation and argument should be abandoned. In fact, it can only arise when the ego arises, for without the "I" thought, there is no "you" thought, which is the world, and there is then no need to account for the world by positing a God-thought as its source. This abidance in the egoless state is "acceptable to all" because, without the ego, I become the all. I become acceptable to myself.

Verse 4

So long as one thinks he has a form,
The world and God too have forms.
When one is the formless Self, who is there to see?
It is itself the eye, complete, limitless.

When I identify with the body, I localize existence and consciousness, or at least I believe they are localized in the physical form I take to be myself. But the body does not contain existence any more than it contains consciousness. The real state of affairs is entirely the reverse: the body appears in the conscious being that I am. I superimpose existence and consciousness on the body and then ascribe the limitations of the body to existence and consciousness. This is called mutual superimposition (*anyonya adhyasa*). It leads to the misunderstanding that it is Vedanta's purpose to correct.

The mistake of identifying our conscious being with a body/mind should be obvious. After all, has existence a particular complexion, height, weight, IQ, etc.? Does consciousness reside at the address where my body resides? Obviously not. But our default position, what is called *dehatma buddhi*, makes this identification all the time. It is a stubborn habit that has persisted from time immemorial.

And because of this habit we believe the world exists apart from us as a collection of separate objects. God, too, becomes a separate object with a form we assign to him based upon our belief. These distinctions all rest on our assuming that we have a limited form. Whatever I perceive is then measured by its distance from that form. And God, of course, is the most distant, for he cannot be perceived in our immediate precinct but is thought to inhabit a timeless place, which is necessarily remote and imaginary.

But when I realize that all forms, including my body and my mind, are perceived by me, then all forms become objects. An object can only exist if there is a subject. The subject is me, my awareness. Can I separate a perceived object from my awareness of it? If I cannot, then subject and object lose their distinction and there is only awareness.

Now, the phrase "my awareness" was just used. This implies that awareness is a property or faculty of something other than awareness. Can there be something other than awareness? Can there be a separate "I" that is aware of awareness? If awareness is needed to be aware of awareness, then we are looking at an infinite regression. And there is no way to divide awareness; only the objects that appear in awareness. And if those objects depend upon awareness, exist in awareness, they, too, cannot be separate from awareness. All divisions are only apparent.

At this point, it might be helpful to resort to the analogy of the clay pot, which Vedanta uses with great effect to explain the truth of non-duality or *advaita* – no second thing. I perceive a pot. The pot is made of clay. Without clay, there is no pot. When I talk about the pot, I am really using a term that can only refer to clay. Yet, the pot cannot be said to be in clay, for clay exists without the pot. The pot, however, does not exist without the clay. What sort of being has the pot? It has an appearance. It is useful. But it has no being in itself. It is name and form, not a substance. It is what is called *mithya* in Vedanta: dependent being.

Now all objects are identical with awareness. They have no being outside of awareness. If I think something exists outside of awareness, I am circumscribing awareness in a physical form. I am thinking of something that may not be in the vicinity of my bodily senses but which nevertheless exists in another location. But in thinking about it, I am aware of it. To say that an object and awareness can be separated is like saying the pot can exist without the clay. No clay, no pot; no pot, still clay. No awareness, no object; no object, still awareness.

Awareness and existence cannot be separated. Ramana says that once we realize this, we recognize the formlessness of our being, even in the presence of form. There remains no "other" to be seen. I am standing here, and you are standing five feet distant from me, but there is one conscious being manifesting as our bodies. We are "the eye of the eye" as the Kena Upanishad expresses it. We never see, think or experience anything that is not the Self. If all of this is giving you a touch of vertigo, it is because the truth is so different from the way we have habitually conceived it that a sense of disorientation can occur when we first hear it. But Ramana continues to explain it in various ways so that we can see the truth from every angle until it becomes our vision, our *Sat-Darshanam*.

Verse 5

The body is made up of five sheaths.
The body and the world co-exist.
Can anyone see the world
Unless he has a body?

Ramana is always directing our attention away from the perception of objects – the world – toward the source of perception – the conscious being we call the Self. Here, Ramana refers to the five sheaths that constitute the body as described in the texts of Vedanta. If you have not encountered this information before, the five sheaths are, beginning from the grossest and proceeding to the subtlest: the physical body, the energy body, the mental body, the intellectual body and the causal body.

The only sheath available for direct perception is the physical body, called the food sheath. The body is made of food, which comes from the earth, and returns to food when it decomposes. Its life comes from its physiological functions, which depend upon the breath, prana. Our perception of objects arises from the senses, whose data is coordinated by the mind. How we interact with objects is decided by the intellect. And the innate tendencies which influence the intellect reside in the causal body. All five sheaths are integrated; their distinction is epistemological and used only to demonstrate that neither separately nor collectively can they be the Self. This is taken up in great detail in Shankara's *Vivekachudamini*, which is perhaps the best text for the beginning student of Vedanta.

Ramana says that without the body, consisting of these sheaths, there is no world. This may seem incorrect at first glance. A remote forest does not disappear if there is no human being present to perceive it, we might think. But we can only imagine such a forest through the medium of our senses and the memories they provide. It is our senses that give objects their qualities. Galileo recognized this and concluded that all sense perceptions are necessarily conditioned by the instrument of perception and, therefore, relative rather than absolute. This was another of his dangerous discoveries.

In his *The Nature of Man According to the Vedanta,* John Levy offers the following wonderful passage: "When a something is cognized, a something does certainly exist, but not as it appears, for the appearance is determined solely by the percipient and not by the thing in itself. The senses are like so many languages, which express in their own idiom the unobjectified being that is beyond the domain of expression."

Ramana is not saying that we personally create the world, but that the perception of the world as we know it cannot occur without a bodily presence. This is easily verified. When we are in deep sleep, we no longer perceive the world because the other bodily sheaths resolve into the causal body. Everything that was manifest in waking and dream becomes unmanifest. But it remains in seed form. When we awake, when bodily awareness returns, the world returns. The seed sprouts. The body and the world then arise simultaneously.

Ramana is not here addressing the question of *Ishwara,* or God, as that which manifests the world, including all individual body/minds. He is focusing on the *jiva,* the individual. And he is simply stating the fact that an individual perception of the world cannot occur without a body.

Verse 6

The world is in the form of five-fold senses, like sound.
These senses are known through the five sense organs.
The mind alone perceives the world through these sense organs.
Therefore, the world is but the mind.

When we are reading, we sometimes realize that we have not understood the words our eyes have just seen. There is nothing wrong with our eyes, and the passage may be simple to understand. The lack of comprehension results from our mind no longer being focused on the impressions being delivered to it by the sense of sight. We say, "I was distracted" or "I was absent-minded." The latter expression demonstrates the truth Ramana is presenting to us in this verse: sense perception depends ultimately on the mind.

Ramana begins by saying that the world is in the form of the senses. We explored this fact in the previous verse. Sound does not exist independently of the sense of hearing, and the same is true of all the perceived qualities that collectively form what we call the world. But nothing is perceived without the mind, which coordinates sense data into a unified impression, that is, into a form to which we then give a name. When Vedanta refers to the world as *namarupa* – name and form – this is what is meant.

The world, then, is the collection of names and forms comprised by the mind through the medium of the sense organs. Even what we call abstract thoughts have some basis in sense knowledge and its lexicon. Ramana is again drawing our attention to the fact that the world, which we take to be away from us, is really nothing other than our mental modifications.

Again, we must not make the mistake of thinking that the world is the product of our individual mind. As we will see later, the individual mind does not exist apart from the total manifestation we call *Ishwara*. Our perception is limited, but the world that arises in that perception appears in the mind: it is a thought modification. This is what Ramana is saying in this verse. As far as the individual is concerned, the world is mind. It is just that the mind of the *jiva* – the individual – does not encompass the mind of *Ishwara*, the total.

Verse 7

Even though both the mind and the world rise and set together.
It is the mind which lights the world.
The source from which the world and the mind arise and into
which they set
Is the Reality, which does not rise or subside.

When Ramana refers to the mind, he means the "I" thought, for every perception occurs in the mind of a conscious being. I am that conscious being. If I say, "This is a table," I am saying that I exist and that a table is known by me. The world, then, is known by me, and without me, it is not known. When the "I" thought is resolved in deep sleep, the world disappears with it. When the "I" thought returns upon waking, the world returns with it.

The world and the "I" thought always appear together, and if one is absent, the other is absent. This is called invariable concomitance. It's a very useful piece of logic that can be formulated as: if A, then B; if no A, then no B. If I am here, the world is here; if I am not here, the world is not here. Again, we should bear in mind that Ramana is talking about the individual, the *jiva*.

Now, the important question is: If the "I" thought and the world rise and set together, where do they come from and where do they go? Recall that the definition of Reality is that which cannot be negated in past, present or future. Anything that rises and sets is a creature of time and not real in the absolute sense. So, both the "I" thought and the world must be dependent realities, what is called *mithya*. That on which they depend is the focus of our inquiry, the true "I," which Ramana calls Reality.

This Reality, however, must be distinguished from that which comes and goes until it is seen clearly, and our vision of it is firm. The verses continue to bring us to that vision.

Verse 8

Worship of the Supreme in any name and in any form
Is an aid for the vision of it.
True vision, however, is merging
And abiding in the Reality.

There is a prevalent notion that Vedanta is but one of many paths that lead to Self-knowledge. Swami Vivekananda is largely responsible for this. He visited America more than a century ago and was a popular and charismatic speaker. He taught that we can choose from a variety of *yogas* the one most suited to our personal inclinations: *jnana yoga* for the intellectual; *bhakti yoga* for the emotional; *karma yoga* for the active; and *raja yoga* for the meditative. Or we can mix and match.

With the appearance in the West of many gurus from India during the past 50 years, there has also arisen what might be called a spiritual-practices supermarket. The confusion resulting from so many self-proclaimed enlightened beings, many with their own method or teaching, has been exacerbated by the internet, where everything is instantly available. There are even websites that promise online *shaktipat*: the transmission of grace from guru to disciple that is supposed to awaken one's dormant spiritual energy.

When Ramana was writing, however, the situation for one seeking self-knowledge was less complicated. Still, there were those who believed that devotion to a deity, or the practice of meditation, were sufficient to free one from the "I" feeling that identifies with what comes and goes and results in the pain of repeated loss and disappointment. Ramana tells us in this verse that all *sadhanas* – spiritual paths – other than self-inquiry can only be aids to self-knowledge. Why should this be so?

Let's consider *bhakti*, the path of devotion. A frequently

voiced criticism of Vedanta is that it is too intellectual and does not appeal to the heart, which wants to feel something, not just to know something. Those who follow the path of devotion require an object of devotion: this is called an *ishta devata*, a chosen deity. The object of devotion can be a person, living or dead, as well as an image of a god or goddess. Some people choose Ramana, who died in 1950. This is a rather safe thing for the ego, or "I" thought, as it can remain in control of the relationship, which exists in imagination. Christians can construct a similar relationship with Jesus.

Now, if the true Self is "free of thoughts," as Ramana tells us at the beginning of *Sat-Darshanam*, then spiritual practices that nurture thoughts about someone who is not us, no matter how sublime or loving these thoughts may be, will not allow us to rest in knowledge of the true Self; It will leave us rooted in the devotional "I" thought. We become devotees. And really, whatever thoughts we have about our object of devotion are really thoughts about who we want to become, about an identity we hope to acquire in time. God, for most of us, is but an ideal version of ourselves.

If we choose a sadhana that is more concerned with particular practices, such as *raja yoga*, we must learn a great many things about how to breathe and how to sit and how to manage our mind in meditation. And our aim will be to become a yogi: one who can remain in *samadhi* for extended periods. But *samadhi* will end when we open our eyes and resume our lives. So, we will have created a practice that, in effect, divorces us from the normal run of our lives and from other people and which has as its aim the enjoyment of states that are time-bound, like any other experience.

Ramana says that worship and yoga can help us toward knowledge of the Self, but it is only "merging and abiding" in that Reality that is the true vision. Now, the use of the word "merging" can be misunderstood, as it suggests that there are two things that must become one. If this were the case, then *bhakti* or *raja* yoga might be alternatives to Vedanta. But merging here can only mean giving up the notion that we are separate from the Self. It is not a question of taking the "I" notion with its bundle of identities and joining it to a new identity. It is losing the "I" notion entirely that allows us to abide in Reality, that is, the Self that is "free of thoughts."

Ramana wants us to ask ourselves: who is it who worships or who does yoga? His intention is always to turn us away from objects and toward the light in which objects are known; away from the "I" thought and toward that which illumines the thought.

Devotion to a deity or assiduous practice of yoga can help weaken our attachment to certain "I" thoughts. When we are worshiping our chosen deity, we are not thinking about our body. When we are meditating, we are not immersed in thoughts about objects, about our likes and dislikes. These practices help clear the mind of a great many "I" thoughts that are obstacles to knowing who we are. But they cannot take us to who we are, because there is no path to the Self. We are already there.

Actions such as worship and meditation produce states of mind that come and go. But the mind, no matter how blissful, loving or peaceful its state, is not the Self. We are. This is difficult to accept, but it is all there is to Vedanta. Ramana is really saying the same thing in each verse, but he is showing us the truth from several different angles, so that we can see it from wherever we may be.

Verse 9

When the individual, for whom duality and trinity exist,
Is traced, they loosen and fall.
Then all mental movement
Ceases forever.

Those practices mentioned in the previous verse involve, in the case of devotion, a worshiper and the object of worship; in the case of yoga, the practice, the practitioner and the goal of practice. Ramana wants us to consider not just the act of devotion or the practice of yoga, but the one who is aware of these actions and for whose benefit they are performed.

Before I perform an act of worship, I am there. During the act of worship, I am there. After the act of worship, I am there. No matter how often I think lovingly of my chosen deity, I am there before the thought arises, while the thought persists, and after the thought dissolves. Before I meditate, I am there. While I meditate, I am there. After I meditate, I am there. So, the individual for whom all these things are done, by whom all of these things are witnessed, is not affected by any of these actions. That one is always present; it is the actions and the states they produce that come and go.

When we realize this, our attention shifts from the actions to the being that is present to all the actions. We realize that the Self, the "I," is not to be found through worship of a deity, or through *samadhi*. That Self is already here. It cannot be gained or lost; increased or decreased; made better or worse. When the mind is peaceful, it witnesses the peace. When the mind is disturbed, it witnesses the disturbance. But it is not peaceful or disturbed. It doesn't change. When Ramana talks about mental movement coming to an end, he does not mean that the mind will stop producing thoughts, but that we will no longer chase after them, hoping to find our Self in the ceaseless flux of mental states. Mental movement will end in the sense that we will remain identified with the stable Self, not with the shifting "I" thoughts that we previously believed to define our being.

Verse 10

Can there be knowledge without ignorance?
Can ignorance exist without knowledge?
Searching the source of the individual to whom they pertain
And abiding there is true knowledge.

Why do we want to know things? What do we hope to find? Something we lack. We believe that out there, in the world, among the variety of objects and experiences, we can find something that will make us feel complete; something that will banish the nagging sense that we are missing something. We hope that by reading one more book, listening to one more series of lectures, gathering a greater mass of information, this painful feeling of inadequacy will give way to a sense of sufficiency, and our ignorance will be replaced by knowledge that will bring lasting satisfaction.

But the knowledge we can acquire about objects, about the world, even about who we think we are, is of the most unstable kind, for it is about things that come and go. No sooner do we master one bit of knowledge, then progress renders it obsolete; or we begin a course of study only to discover how much we don't know. Our newly acquired knowledge, instead of banishing our ignorance, has revealed its vastness. And should we try to understand our personality, we discover how shifting and unpredictable are our moods and thoughts and how difficult it is to identify their source. Some people undergo years of expensive therapy in an attempt to understand and master their minds and emotions, with disappointing results.

Ramana says that knowledge and ignorance are mutually dependent, which means that knowledge can never banish ignorance. He is talking about objective knowledge. When we look at objects, we assume that they have a separate existence and, in the case of sentient beings, a separate consciousness; that they are somehow self-sufficient. We attribute our own being and consciousness to objects and then try to find ourselves through those objects, as though somewhere deep in matter or thought or feeling is the key to the mystery of our identity. It is a bit like analyzing the glass in the mirror to discover the nature of the image it reflects. Objects, like the mirror, are inert. Any sentiency they seem to possess belongs to us.

Now, recall what Swami Parmarthananda says about perception: it is existence – the E-principle – plus an object. Existence is called *satyam*, and it cannot be divided or contained by an object. All objects are names that we give to perceptions. These names are what we call knowledge. And every name can be reduced to other names. A tree can become bark and roots and branches and leaves; and these in turn can become cellulose and chlorophyll and minerals; and these can be broken down into molecules, which can be broken down into cells, which can be broken down into atoms, which can be broken down into particles, which can be broken down into sub-particles. Where does it end? And what have we gained so far in the process? Real knowledge, or a proliferation of names?

Naming something doesn't really tell us what it is. We can even amend Swami Parmarthananda's formula and say the perception is the E-principle plus a name. But it is the E-principle that is real, not the name.

So, when we use the names of objects or experiences to define who we are, we are confusing the E-principle with words and meanings that have no existence apart from it. We are the E-principle. Everything is the E-principle. And everything is known, for existence and knowledge are the same thing. To say that something exists is to say it is known. To name something is to apply a word to this existence/known-ness. But the name does not change existence/known-ness. It does not affect it in any way.

This existence/known-ness is the true "I," the heart of my

being that Ramana spoke about in the opening verse. If I am ignorant of who I am, no amount of object knowledge will take away this ignorance. To look for the Self by acquiring object knowledge (and thoughts and feelings are objects) is like using your flashlight to find your flashlight. It's in your hand all the time: it's the light with which you are looking for the light. It's a rather funny situation.

To know who I am requires that I have an appropriate means of knowledge. And Vedanta is that means. In the Chandogya Upanishad, a student returns home after 12 years of studying the Vedas; he is very proud of all he has learned. His father sees his son's arrogance and asks him, "Did you ask your teacher for that knowledge, knowing which, all else is as good as known?" The young man's vanity and self-assurance is shaken. He says his teacher must not have had this knowledge, for he surely would have given it to his prize student. But it may have been the case that the boy was not yet prepared to receive such knowledge. He then asks his father to teach it to him. And so begins a series of instructions, each lesson ending with the phrase, "That thou art" – *Tat twam asi*.

Ramana in this verse tries to get us to shift our attention away from the knowledge of objects and toward the "I" for whom knowledge exists. Who is knowledgeable? Who is ignorant? Is there a knowing Self and an ignorant Self? Or is there just one conscious being who knows what the mind knows and what it doesn't know and is the ground of both knowledge and ignorance? Look to that source of the "I" who knows and doesn't know and abide there, Ramana says. This is true knowledge, the light in which all is known. "That thou art."

Verse 11

Can knowledge of everything, without Self-knowledge,
Be true knowledge?
Awareness of the Self, which is the support of knower and known,
Destroys the pair, knowledge and ignorance.

No matter how vast our total knowledge may be, the mind can hold only one thought at a time. It may seem that we can think of several things simultaneously, but this is due to the speed with which thoughts come and go. To know a particular thing means that I must hold the thought of it in my mind for a time. This also means that I must then become ignorant of all other thoughts during that time. I cannot think of you if I am thinking of the Pythagorean Theorem. One thought always displaces the previous thought. So, each thought requires ignorance of other thoughts. This is why knowledge and ignorance are mutually dependent.

When I hold a thought in my mind, that thought is an image of an object, even if it is a feeling or an abstract concept. For that image to appear, a reflecting medium must be present. This reflecting medium is the mind. The mind's reflection of an object, in turn, depends upon awareness. Awareness is what lights up the mind and allows images to appear in it.

We make the mistake of thinking the situation is reversed: that images light up the mind, or that the mind is self-shining. But neither Vedanta nor experience bears this out. The Kena Upanishad says that awareness is the "eye of the eye." In other words, it is that which enables the sense organ of sight to present objects to the mind. We know this is so, because there is no inherent power of awareness in the eyes. My eyes can be looking at one thing, but my mind may be reflecting something else – a thought, a memory; and I am then not aware of what my eyes are seeing.

When I was a boy, opinions about my intelligence were mixed, mostly due to my absent-mindedness. I once walked into a tree during an outing with my family. My mother, while dabbing my bleeding nose, asked in exasperation, "Didn't you see that tree?" I didn't know what to answer. Of course, I saw the tree, but I was not aware of it. The appropriate answer would have been, "Yes, my eyes saw the tree, but my mind was reflecting a different thought, so my mind didn't see what my eyes saw."

And we know that every night, our mind goes away for a time. But its absence and the consequent disappearance of reflected objects does not result in our disappearance. We somehow persist and, when we awake, the parade of reflections resumes.

So, neither the objects, nor the senses, nor the mind are the source of true knowledge. It is awareness, and that awareness is me. Any object that is reflected in the mind, including all the "I" thoughts, e.g., I am fat, I am stupid, I am hungry, I feel sad, etc., depend entirely upon the light of awareness. Realizing this is true knowledge, which creates nothing and changes nothing; it merely removes the ignorance that kept the always present truth obscured.

When we realize that the mind is not the knower, but the medium of reflection, and that all that is appears in awareness, and is awareness, then true knowledge is recognized. Without this knowledge, no amount of object knowledge can remove our ignorance.

Verse 12

Neither sleep nor the cognition of objects is knowledge.
In the true state, which is different from both,
There is no awareness of objects, but consciousness alone shines.
Hence it is not a void.

When I perceive objects as separate from me, I regard them as separate from consciousness. But no object is separate from consciousness, which is to say, no object can exist as separate from me.

The cognition of objects that Ramana says is not true knowledge involves the intellect taking hold of an object. This process is described by the Sanskrit word, *grahanam*, which means "grasping." When I cognize an object, I grasp it by giving the image that appears in my intellect a name. But in doing so, I have divorced that object from all other objects, to which I have given different names. I have also divorced it from the consciousness from which it is formed. I am left with a name, which I think represents an entity distinct from the consciousness in which it subsists.

A dictionary is a list of names for supposedly distinct objects. Our memories are really dictionaries, lists of names for all the things that take shape in consciousness. The list is useful to us as we go about our business in the world, but it cannot help us to discover that which is real; that which we truly are.

Recall the analogy of the pot and the clay. The pot has no being in itself. It is clay through and through. Pot is a name for a form that has no ontological reality, to use a philosophic term. It is, to use a Vedantic term, *mithya*: dependent being. All the objects that can be grasped and named are *mithya*. So, what is the ground of *mithya*? What is the clay of the pot? Consciousness. Which is me.

To realize that I am consciousness and that all perceptions depend upon me is true knowledge.

But we have a deeply ingrained orientation to think of consciousness as involving two things: a subject and an object. Does consciousness exist without an object to be grasped? In deep sleep, there are no objects to be grasped, no *grahanam*; so, there can be no mistaken perception of objects as separate from my consciousness. But the mere absence of object knowledge is not true knowledge. I may have no mistaken knowledge about calculus, because I know nothing of calculus. But I cannot say that the absence of mistaken knowledge is true knowledge.

Some Vedanta teachers equate deep sleep with non-dual knowledge because of the absence of subject and object. In making this equation, they miss something crucial in Vedanta: an experience of non-duality is not the same as the knowledge of non-duality. This is why *samadhi*, in which the subject and object disappear, can be a means for purifying the mind but cannot be a means of knowledge. *Samadhi*, despite its attractions and benefits, is ultimately a time-bound experience: it isn't there, then it's there, then it isn't there.

This has been mentioned previously but it bears repeating, for confusion about this distinction has led to serious misunderstanding about the nature of Vedanta as a means of knowledge. There is a persistent notion that the truth Vedanta proclaims needs to be verified by experience. This notion makes meditation the means of knowledge for *moksha*, liberation. It regards the Upanishads as records of experiences certain individuals had in meditation; and it is maintained that only through these experiences can the teaching become direct knowledge. The Upanishads then become dispensable. They can, at best, be only an indirect means of knowledge. This notion, though very popular, is opposed to the teaching of Vedanta, which understands all experiences as objects and, therefore, as time-bound and ultimately unreal.

Ramana tells us in this verse that true knowledge is realizing that consciousness alone shines, and this self-shining consciousness is not affected by the presence of objects or their absence. When no objects are present, consciousness does not become a void. When objects are present, consciousness remains unaffected. It is the light that is changeless and, therefore, timeless. That which comes and goes appears in this self-shining light.

Verse 13

Consciousness, the Self, is real.
The many forms cannot exist apart from it.
Can the different ornaments exist by themselves?
Are they apart from gold?

Can any thought be known unless I know it? Can any object be perceived unless I perceive it? And every thought that is known will soon be replaced by another thought. Every object perceived will soon be replaced by another object and another perception. All thoughts and perceptions depend upon me. They come and go, but I – consciousness – remain.

And the "I" that remains is unaffected by the slide show of the mind. This "I" is the knower and it is entirely independent of the known, just as the light in the projector is independent of the images it illumines. But the known is entirely dependent upon the knower. What's more, the knower does not actually perform an act of knowing: it simply reveals what exists and what cannot exist apart from it. The light in the projector need not do anything to illumine the images on the film; it is the unchanging medium that reveals all that passes in front of it.

So, when we say consciousness is the knower, we are not being entirely accurate, as the statement implies that some action is needed on the part of consciousness to reveal what is known. There are not actually two things – knower and known – but consciousness alone. Knower and known do not represent a genuine ontological division; only an epistemological one. This will be taken up in greater detail in the next verse.

Ramana relies on one of Vedanta's most often used analogies for the non-dual nature of reality: gold and ornaments. Different ornaments – ring, bracelet, necklace, bangle, etc. – do not exist apart from the gold of which they are made. If you try to sell several ornaments to a pawn broker, he will put them on a scale and value them according to their weight, not their form. Form doesn't matter to him: forms are mere names for what is simply gold.

The various thoughts and perceptions that come and go in the mind are nothing other than consciousness. They cannot exist without it. Their different forms ultimately depend upon the ground of their being, which is the unchanging awareness from which they arise, in which they remain for a time, and into which they resolve. They have no separate existence, just as the various ornaments have no existence separate from gold.

Verse 14

Without the "I" the second and third persons cannot exist.
When the "I" subsides through inquiry about its source,
The second and third persons too disappear.
Our own natural state shines forth.

When an object is known, it appears in consciousness, from which it cannot be separated, just as ornaments cannot be separated from the gold of which they are made. When something is perceived, the sense instruments collect data which they transmit to the mind; the mind then forms an impression based on this information and gives that impression a name. But who is the knower of the name?

If I say, "I see this computer screen," who is the "I"? It's true that information about size, shape, color, texture, etc., has been collected and collated into an impression and assigned a name, but who is the "I" to whom I attribute the act of seeing? The eyes? The internal sense organ in the brain? Is there a separate being who exists apart from this process of cognition and who is superintending it?

The computer screen is seen, but there is no "I" involved in the seeing: only consciousness. There is no other "I." Yet, consciousness is not what we generally mean when we say "I." We rather mean a number of things that have to do with perceptions about the body, emotions, memories, desires, fears – a vast and complex array of images that appear in consciousness in the same way the computer screen appears. The difference between the screen perception and the "I" thoughts is that I do not think I am a computer screen. I do think I am 5 feet, 10 inches, 180 pounds, a man with a history of relationships and memories of actions performed by the body I take myself to be. But these "I" thoughts are objectified, just as the screen is objectified. This can only mean the "I" thoughts are not me, for I can never be an object to myself. That would require that there be a second me to perceive the first me and so on, *ad infinitum*.

Ramana is telling us in this verse that all objectification has its origin in this objectification of the "I." Ramana says that as soon as we perceive our Self to be separate from consciousness, we perceive the world to be separate from us. As soon as I say "I," it necessarily follows that there must be "you" and "that."

But if I investigate the nature of the "I" thought, it becomes but another object of perception. Who then is the perceiver? It cannot be one of the objects perceived. It must be that in which all objects are perceived: me, consciousness.

It might be good at this point to say something about what is commonly called level confusion as it is wont to occur in the study of Vedanta. When Ramana, following the Upanishads, says that consciousness is the true "I" and that there is only consciousness, he is not suggesting that the world is a projection of our consciousness as individual beings. You will hear it sometimes said in spiritual circles, "We create the world," or some such statement.

We – you and I – do not create the world. We, as individuals, are born into the world, which existed before we arrived and will continue to exist after we depart. The world, the collectivity of all objects, including us, is a manifestation (*shristi*) of *Ishwara*, the creative intelligence of *Brahman*. The power by which *Ishwara* manifests objects is called *maya*.

When Ramana says that with the subsidence of the "I" thought, the second and third persons disappear, he is not talking about any alteration that will occur in *Ishwara shristi*, which is the objective order that we commonly perceive; he is talking about a change in *jiva shristi*, which is the subjective order. When we no longer see ourselves as the "I" thoughts that separate us from other people and the world as well as from what we consider to be God, we will have true knowledge. It is not that anything will change in the objective order: it will all appear the same as it did before we came to true knowledge. The change will be that we will see ourselves as we are, not as we wrongly supposed ourselves to be. The change is a mental change.

Shankara, in his commentary on the Chandogya Upanishad, says, "non-dual realization is a mere mental modification." The use of the word "mere" might not convey how profoundly this realization affects the one who comes to it, but it does make clear that it does not involve any change in the objective order, which is an expression of *Ishwara's* knowledge, not our imagination or projection.

And as the objective order is a manifestation of *Ishwara's* knowledge, we, too, are a manifestation of *Ishwara's* knowledge. We are not the cause of the objective order; we are the effect of that order. What a wonderful relief it is to realize this. To express the realization as a correction of level confusion, we can say that we are not *Ishwara*, but *Ishwara* is us. This means we can relax and stop thinking that we must manage the creation. This is *moksha* – liberation.

Verse 15

In their time, both past and future are only the present.
Is it not a matter of laughter to debate
About past and future, unaware of the present?
Can one count without the number one?

Ramana now wants us to reflect on who we are by considering the nature of time. We tend to define ourselves by our history. But all that occurred in the past occurred in what was then the present. And all that is occurring now is occurring in the present. Likewise, all that will occur in the future will occur in what will then be the present. There is really only the present. What is past and future then? Can it be other than the present?

When we remember something, we do not go back in time to the moment when the recollected event happened. We think about it now. There is no past existence. And when we project ourselves into the future, we do so in present imagination. There is no future existence. And when something happens now, we say that it exists in the present. But all exists in the present, including what we call past and future, for there is no other time than the present. Existence is not divided by time.

Ramana then takes us a step further: he says it is ridiculous to imagine that time can be divided in any way, for even the present cannot be located and measured. If we try to say, "Now I am in the present," no sooner do we say it, then the "Now" we just referred to is no longer present. Its place has been usurped by a new "Now." We are just not quick enough to catch and keep the "Now." For the "Now" is a thought, and thoughts come and go with the speed of light.

In my distant youth, which I am thinking of in the present, there was a popular spiritual book titled, *Be Here Now.* I remember very little about its contents, but it was understood by its devotees to mean that we should try to avoid thinking about the past or the future.

Now, it is undeniable that much anguish is caused by our sorrowing over the past and fretting about the future. We think, "If only I had done this instead of that, all would be different now." And we worry about what will happen tomorrow, or next week, or next year: "Will I get what I want? Will I get what I don't want? Will I sell my house? Will I find my soul mate? Will I make a million dollars? Will I go bankrupt? Will I get cancer?" The litany of regrets, longings and forebodings is never-ending.

Those who exhort us to be here now propose that we bring an end to this painful litany by an exercise of the will: we are to fix ourselves in the present.

But how can we fix ourselves in the present? To do so would require that the present be a constant location in space and time. And who is to occupy this fixed point of the present? Am I different in the present than I am in the past or the future? Is there any way of divorcing myself from the present and occupying a different point in time? Am I not always in the present? Do I have to make an effort to be in the present?

It is true that to define ourselves by the past or project ourselves into the future is to live in imagination based on experience, either actual or anticipated. And Ramana's point is that we are not to be defined by experiences, which are time-bound, because we are the unchanging witness of those experiences. The present "I," the past "I," and the future "I" are the same "I." Time appears in awareness as the succession of thoughts. Thoughts change, but awareness remains constant. Thoughts are creatures of time. Awareness is timeless.

We cannot help but *Be Here Now*. We are the *Now*. This is really the point of Vedanta. We cannot do anything to become something we presently are not. To try to fix the mind on a thought and keep it there is a meditation practice. To the extent that we succeed in this practice, we can enjoy a relatively peaceful mind. But who is it who enjoys this temporary state? Is it not the same consciousness that was present before meditation, during meditation and after meditation?

In the previous verse, Ramana dispensed with the division of the world that comes about through thinking we are separate from all that we perceive, as though consciousness can be divided by the use of the pronouns: I, you, it. Now, Ramana is saying that consciousness cannot be divided by time, because time occurs in consciousness, not the other way around. The awareness we are is the ground, the *adhisthana*, of time as it is of all that is *mithya* – all that has a dependent and not an absolute existence.

Swami Dayananda used to tell students that he was teaching them Vedanta mathematics, in which 1 + 1 = 1. Ramana is doing the same in this verse when he asks whether it is possible to count without the number 1? There is really only one number – 1 – just as there is really only timeless awareness. You cannot add anything to awareness, nor subtract anything from awareness. It is simply the unchanging light in which all things appear, including the thoughts of past, present and future.

Verse 16

Can there be space, can there be time, except for me?
Space and time bind me only if I am the body.
I am nowhere, I am timeless,
I exist everywhere and always.

Space is the distance between two objects. Space has no content and is not absolute, but relative. Time is the interval between two thoughts. It has no content and is not absolute, but relative. I am aware of space and time only in relation to objects and thoughts. When there are no objects or thoughts, as in deep sleep or *samadhi,* space and time disappear, but I remain. I am the awareness in which both appear and disappear.

And in the waking and dream states, objects and thoughts appear in space and time, either objectively, in our shared reality, or subjectively, in our individual imagination. But all objects and thoughts (and objects are actually thoughts) are known by me – the conscious being. I persist in the space between objects; I persist in the interval between thoughts. If this were not so, I would have no sense of continuity and my identity would completely change with each changing thought.

Now, if I am the body, then my existence depends upon the body, as does my consciousness, for there is no consciousness without existence. But if I were the body, then consciousness would be bound by my physical form, as though the body were a container for consciousness. This is, in fact, what some materialists believe. But this is not borne out by my experience. In dream and deep sleep, the physical form is not present in consciousness.

If consciousness were limited by the body, then there must be some material that generates and maintains consciousness. The brain is usually put forth as a candidate for this function.

But the brain can only be shown to be an instrument for sense perception, and even saying that much is problematic as it contains many unproven assumptions. And, according to such a theory, the instrument by which we are examining brain function is none other than the brain. This presents us with the problem of having no objective criteria for such a study. Can the brain assess the brain? Can the eye look at the eye? Can the ear hear the ear?

But space and time can only appear in our awareness when we identify with the body. In fact, both concepts require more than one body or one thought. Space only comes into being when a second body appears and then is known as the distance between the two bodies. Time only comes into being when there is a second thought and then is known as the interval between the two thoughts. Duality is the essence of space and time.

Now, if there were only one body and one thought, there could be no measure of space and time. Consciousness, although it is neither a body nor a thought, is indivisible. If it were divisible, there would have to be some break in existence where non-existence intervened, and non-existence would mean non-awareness. From this nothingness, existence/awareness would have to re-emerge, which is clearly impossible. Curiously, much so-called scientific thought assumes such an impossibility, for materialists have placed existence/awareness inside physical containers and must somehow account for the division of such containers, which means they must posit non-existence and non-awareness as real, which is contradictory.

If I am existence/awareness, and not a body, then space and time do not apply to me. I cannot be located here and not there, or at this time and not at another time. I am everywhere and nowhere; at all times and at no time.

Verse 17

Both the wise and ignorant regard the body as "I."
The ignorant limit the "I" to the body.
For the wise, the Self shines in the heart,
Limitless, including the body and the world.

If I am not the body, why do I identify my Self with the body? The fact is, I am the body; that is, the conscious being I am includes the body, as it includes all objects. So, it is not entirely correct to say that I am not the body.

I naturally feel that I am the body because, in a certain sense, it is true, just as it is true to say that a pot is indeed clay; but one cannot say that clay is a pot, just as one cannot say that existence/awareness is a body. When the pot is no more, clay remains. When the body is no more, existence/awareness remains.

The ignorant person, that is, one who does not know who he really is, assumes that his conscious being is co-terminus with his physical form. He fears death, along with all the ills that can befall the body. He is tortured on the rack of time in which his body grows older and nears its day of extinction. He foresees his bodily death and the void opens before him, filling his mind with terror.

Now, the same bodily fate awaits the one who knows he is the existence/awareness in which the body appears and lives out its appointed time. He answers to the name given the body; eats, works, sleeps, procreates, sickens and dies like those who do not know they are existence/awareness. But he does not live in fear. He does not fret over the inevitable physical demise that is the common destiny of all physical forms. That which is composed of the elements will necessarily decompose in time. But existence/awareness is not composed of earth, water, fire or air. It is not an object in space. But it shines in all objects as their very being and known-ness.

This timeless existence/awareness is the heart Ramana spoke of in the opening prayer verse. And it is this heart that the wise person knows to be the Self; not the body. But the body only exists because the Self exists. It is only known because the Self is known. It depends entirely upon the Self, which is completely independent of it. The body is, in a word, *mithya*. This is what the wise know and what the ignorant fail to realize.

Verse 18

To the ignorant and for the wise, the world exists.
The ignorant regard the world alone as real.
For the wise, the formless source of the seen
Is real, complete.

The world of common perception is called in Vedanta *vyavaharika*. If there is a tree in front of two people who are standing close together, both will see the tree in the same way in terms of its physical characteristics. *Vyavahaika* knowledge conforms to the object and is accessible to all who have the requisite sense organs.

What each person thinks about the tree, however, may differ: one may regard it aesthetically, as a beautifully formed piece of nature; the other may regard it as potential firewood or building material. The differing appreciations of the tree have to do with another level of perception called *pratibhasika*. *Pratibhasika* is subjective and arises from individual characteristics of mind and experience, not shared perceptions of objects.

There is, however, a third level of knowledge called *paramarthika* in which both objective and individual perceptions resolve into awareness, which is really what they are. In fact, some texts of Vedanta don't bother to distinguish between *vyavaharika* and *pratibhasika*, as both types of perception are nothing other than awareness with name and form superimposed. Recall Swami Parmarthananda's E-principle-plus-the-object formula. Whether the object is commonly perceived or individually perceived, it remains dependent on existence/awareness. In fact, it is nothing other than existence/awareness plus the name and form.

The ignorant look at the world and see a variety of objects, as do the wise. But the ignorant superimpose upon the objects a distinct and independent existence. They see the pot and take the pot to be real, without recognizing that the pot is just clay. The wise see the pot as clay through and through. Pot, they regard as a name – one of many possible names (plate, bowl, vase, etc.) – that signify the same thing: clay.

Westerners who come to explore Eastern spirituality often acquire strange ideas connected with words such as enlightenment and liberation. They read texts that say that for the enlightened one, the world is no more, and they imagine that it is possible to achieve a state of perception which is radically different from what ordinary people enjoy. The conventional world does not disappear for the enlightened; they simply see it from the standpoint of unchanging awareness. They are rooted in *paramarthika* knowledge.

The snake and the rope can be pressed into service here. A traveler sees what he believes to be a snake lying across his path in the twilight. Another comes by and points out that what the first person believed to be a snake is really a rope. The first person had *pratibhasika* knowledge which was corrected by *vyavaharika* knowledge. But let's suppose a third person comes along and explains that the rope is only a name for a thought form that is wholly dependent upon awareness and cannot be separated from awareness, just as the pot cannot be separated from the clay. He is the wise one who has *paramarthika* knowledge, for he knows the formless source of the seen, which is the Self.

Verse 19

The controversy whether fate is stronger than free will or vice versa,
Is only for those who do not know their source.
Those who know the individual for whom they pertain
Remain untouched by them.

We want to know whether there is justice in the way our lives unfold: are we responsible for our suffering or are we afflicted by arbitrary forces? It is a question of immense importance in the West, where it has been framed historically as a debate about the respective roles of free will and Providence in human affairs. The Protestant Reformation had largely to do with an argument about whether salvation was determined by our voluntary efforts or God's inscrutable will. The argument led to ruinous wars and is yet unresolved.

Even if God is left out of it, the question persists: are we in charge or is someone or something else pulling the strings that move us in particular ways. The atheist writer Albert Camus counseled what he described as metaphysical rebellion. Having decided that human beings can have done nothing to merit the punishments of life, the chief of which are disease and death, he urged us to raise our fists to Heaven and curse God or the fates or whatever is responsible for the sorry plight of mortal man. His message has the romantic appeal of making the young feel they are tragic heroes and heroines in a darkly grand drama.

Camus rejected Christianity and any apologia for a just and rational order of creation. His legacy is a sense of grievance among those who feel they haven't gotten the good things they think they deserve. And someone else, of course, must be blamed. But the champions of free will also endure. They urge people to accept responsibility for their lives: quit grumbling and take charge is their advice to the disaffected.

Ramana tells us in this verse that the argument about whether free will or fate is responsible for our present state of affairs is pointless for one who knows who he is. It is only meaningful for one who believes he is an actor in the world of changing objects. But if the "I" is attached to anything that comes and goes, the "I" will come and go, too, and a sense of continuous identity then becomes impossible. Our sense of identity is really due to the changeless existence/awareness we are, which we superimpose upon objects we then mistakenly take to be the Self. We then act, through the body/mind, in an attempt to become what we already are. Having projected our existence/awareness into the world of objects, we then try to take it back.

When I believe I am the body/mind, I feel small and incomplete and unstable, for I have identified with that which has these characteristics. I then try to do something to compensate for this sense of inadequacy. Action begets more action, and each action is limited by time and space and mires me further in the world of objects. Present action becomes future fate and the wheel of *samsara*, of constant change, keeps turning.

It is only on the *vyavaharika* level, where apparently separate beings interact in the waking state, that free will and fate can have any meaning. For one with *paramarthika* knowledge, all is resolved into the one conscious being in which separateness dissolves. The snake and the rope might help us better understand what Ramana is saying.

Our traveler sees what he thinks is a snake lying across the road in the twilight. Another traveler comes along and is warned by the first traveler about the snake. Soon, more people come along and a group forms. Discussions arise about what sort of snake it might be. Opinions vary. Some even say it may not be a snake, but a streak of water or a crack in the earth. Supporting evidence and logic are offered for the contending positions. Some say the snake has been placed there by fate or Providence; others say its appearance at this particular time and place is gratuitous. There is much talk about how the snake, if it is a snake, might be circumvented or induced to slither away. Some favor a direct assault. Plans are proposed and debated. Fights break out. Then, someone comes along with a flash light and the rope is clearly seen for what it is. What value, then, remains for the mass of argument and speculation that has grown around the non-existent snake?

Actions cause effects in time. So long as we think we are creatures of time, we will try to discover the causes of actions. But when we recognize we are timeless, the search for causes ends. When the rope is seen, we stop wondering about the snake.

Still, on the *vyavaharika,* or empirical, level, a provisional explanation of cause and effect may be helpful, and Vedanta provides one. We should bear in mind that this is what is called an "as though" answer, which underscores its relative nature. As a *jiva,* an individual being, we are born into a set of circumstances at a given time. Whatever choices the *jiva* has are circumscribed by his parentage, upbringing, education, social position and a host of other factors. He may be free to act, but only within the limited range allowed by his conditioning. And those actions will determine future circumstances in which further actions can be taken. So, one can say that free will determines fate, and fate limits free will. Our subjectivity – *pratibhasika* – interacts with and is limited by objectivity – *vyavaharika.*

To ask at what point in time the *jiva* came into being and how his initial birth can have been caused by previous action leads to infinite regress: if birth is the result of karma, when can that karma have been accumulated prior to birth? I cannot have pre-existed myself. The only escape from this absurdity is to recognize that I am not a *jiva* caught in time. The "I" thoughts that situate me in time appear in awareness and have no being apart from awareness. The individual exists "as though" it were real in the world of transient objects. This is the world of ignorance, which is said to have no beginning.

How can ignorance have no beginning? Let's suppose I know nothing of calculus. Then I take a class and my ignorance is dispelled. I can say when my ignorance of calculus ended, but can I say when it began? And ignorance can only be said to end on the *pratibhasika* level.

But all that is *pratibhasika* is *mithya*: it is dependent and time-bound. As it comes and goes, it cannot be said to be real. Free will and fate are concerned with the nature of cause and effect, a time-bound sequence. Ramana says free will and fate are irrelevant where there is no time. And for unchanging existence/ awareness, there is no time.

Verse 20

To see God apart from the seer is only a mental image,
Since God is not separate from the seer.
To abide in the poise of the Self
Is true vision of God.

What is a mental image? When I see something, my senses transmit data to my mind, which then organizes the data into an object and gives it a name. The named object is a mental image. But if my mind is preoccupied, I may not see what is in front of me. My senses may be operating and transmitting the data, but my attention is elsewhere. I can only see what is in my mind, at any given time. And whatever is in my mind is a mental image.

Now, a mental image is an object, even if the image is a thought or feeling or fantasy; the mental image appears to me, the subject, and is different from me. Mental images continuously succeed one another, but the one to whom they appear is never succeeded by another. The "I" before whom the mental images ceaselessly parade never moves.

If I see God, that vision can only be a mental image, for I am having it. I am the subject and the vision is the object. Even if the word "vision" signifies an understanding rather than a sensible form, it remains an object, i.e., a mental image. And as a mental image, God has no permanence. Such a deity, no matter how moving and profoundly we may experience its presence, will come and go, like all objects which appear in the mind. And the mind itself is a mental image: it is seen, so it, too, must be an object. If that is the case, and it cannot be otherwise, then who is the subject? Who is the seer of the mental image? I am.

This "I" cannot be objectified, or it, too, would become a mental image and require another seer; and if that seer could be objectified, it would also require another seer, and so on, *ad infinitum*. The only way to avoid an infinite regress is to recognize that awareness is the seer that is never seen; that is, the seer that can never be objectified.

If I am this seer, and if I cannot be objectified, then anything that can be objectified is not me. Anything I can see, in any sense, cannot be me, but only an object perceived by me. Any God that I can see can only be a mental image, dependent upon my awareness; an object that comes and goes, like all objects.

God signifies that which is timeless, infinite, limitless. Awareness is the only thing that can be indicated by these words. It is the only thing we recognize that does not come and go; it is not circumscribed by time and space; it has no boundaries. We cannot see it. We can only be it.

Ramana says that the only true vision of God is the recognition of our true nature as limitless awareness. All talk of God as anything else is only a mental image. The implications of this truth are far-reaching.

The militant atheists that have arisen in our day have gotten hold of the truth that God, as most religions conceive of deity, is but a mental image. And those who claim to have seen such a God or to have received a commission to speak in his name have lost, or are steadily losing, credibility. Perhaps, for some people, this is a necessary step to the understanding Vedanta offers: that we are the limitless being/awareness that we project onto the world of objects, including the pantheon of divinities that we have worshiped through the ages, and whose existence we now deny or debate.

Verse 21

The Scriptures declare, "see the Self," "see God."
It is not easy to understand these ideas.
Because Self is one, it cannot be seen. How can one see God?
It is only by becoming food to Him.

We may have an ardent desire to know the absolute truth, but without an adequate means of knowledge, this desire will be frustrated. Ramana points out in this verse that the exhortations to see the Self or God that we find in scripture can leave us in great perplexity, as we may have no idea how this is to be done.

The problem arises from the fact that our usual means of knowledge are the senses and the mind. Whenever we want to know something, we set about gathering information about its shape, size, color, weight, location, etc. We try to identify its material and efficient causes. But none of these procedures apply when we want to know the Self or God, for the senses can only be directed at objects, and the mind can only form mental images of objects.

The Self is the subject, not the object. It cannot be known through the senses or the mind. But it is not unknown. In fact, it is the one constant in the world in which objects come and go. It is the awareness in which all things are seen, but that can never itself be seen, because it is the unobjectifiable seer. It cannot be known, because it is known-ness itself.

Can I see awareness? If so, then "I" have to be different from awareness; "I" have to be the subject and awareness, the object. But if awareness is the object, then another awareness will be needed to see it. We will fall into an infinite regress. So, the "I" cannot be different from awareness.

Now, all things that are known are known by awareness. To say that something is known is to say that it exists in awareness. Can anything exist outside of awareness? Existence and awareness are inseparable. All that is known then is nothing other than existence/awareness with a particular name and form.

But the name and form are not separate from existence/ awareness. They can be nothing other than existence/awareness, just as the pot can be nothing other than the clay. So even though it appears that there are many objects in the empirical world, all that we perceive, all that can ever be perceived, is our own Self: existence/awareness superimposed upon an object and given a name. We may say, "This is a table," but it would be more precise to say, "Existence tables." And that is the same as saying, "Consciousness tables." There is only one substantive, but there are many *upadhis*, which are the limiting adjuncts of name and form.

If the Self is existence/awareness, the senses and the mind, which work together to distinguish objects according to attributes, cannot help us to see the Self. The senses and the mind, in fact, are seen in the Self. And the senses and mind are limited to those perceptions the individual instruments produce. My mind is not your mind, my experience is not your experience, etc. And the mind of God is certainly not the mind of the individual; that is, the knowledge that manifests the universe is not my individual knowledge.

So how can I know God? Ramana answers: by knowing the Self. If objects only appear in awareness, which is the subject, and this is true for the individual, the same must be true for what we call God or *Ishwara*. If I cannot be an object, neither can *Ishwara*. If I am the Self of all objects, so is *Ishwara*. As an individual body/mind, I do not possess the universal knowledge of *Ishwara*, but as the objects I know are known in awareness, the objects that *Ishwara* knows are also known in awareness. And awareness cannot be divided. The awareness I am is the awareness you are is the awareness *Ishwara* is. There is no second thing: *advaita*.

But as Ramana says, this is not easy to understand, for our habitual mode of knowledge is sense-based. This is why Vedanta is a *pramana*, a valid means of knowledge about the Self. We have no other means. But Vedanta does not reveal the Self. We know we are conscious beings; but we are unclear about our nature and its relation to the objects we perceive. Vedanta's sole function is to provide us with clarity.

One of the most effective examples Vedanta uses to help us see the Self and see God clearly is the analogy of the dream. When we dream, all of the objects and people in the dream exist in our awareness. We may identify with a particular person in the dream, and that person may engage in actions with other people in the dream, but all the beings and objects in the dream are not separate from us. All exist in our awareness and have no existence apart from our awareness. We are the *Ishwara* of the dream, the Self of the dream. We can see this clearly when we wake up from the dream.

If we are the *Ishwara* of the dream, then *Ishwara* is the *Ishwara* of the waking state. As all in the dream state is the manifestation of our individual knowledge, all in the waking world is the manifestation of *Ishwara's* infinite knowledge. Recall the levels of reality mentioned previously. The dream is *pratibhasika*: individual perception. The objective waking world is *vyavaharika*: common perception. The awareness in which both dream and waking objects are known is *paramarthika*: absolute existence/consciousness.

When Ramana says we can only "see God" by becoming "food to Him," what can he mean? He is evoking the image of the temple, where offerings are made to the deity and are often poured into the sacrificial fire. When we realize that all objects are manifestations of *Ishwara's* knowledge, including our body/mind, we no longer lay claim to them. We can offer them to *Ishwara*, to whom they rightfully belong. Then, we will be free of identifying the "I" with that which comes and goes in the mind, and we can rest in the awareness that is changeless and that is the same in me, in you, and in *Ishwara*.

Verse 22

God illumines the mind and shines within it, unseen.
How then can one know God through the mind?
Turning the mind inward and fixing it in Him
Alone is to have His vision.

What is the mind? This may appear a large and daunting question, but fundamentally the mind is a succession of images based on sense perception. The sense instruments are located in the body, and that which coordinates sense data is the brain. But neither the sense instruments nor the brain possesses the power of awareness. They are inert matter, and when consciousness departs, they decompose into the elements from which they are made.

Ramana says that God illumines the mind, which means that the mind has no intrinsic awareness. It reflects awareness, which is the nature of the conscious being we call God or *Ishwara*. This reflected awareness is usually turned outward toward objects (feelings, thoughts and memories, though seemingly internal, are also perceived and, therefore, classed as objects). The Katha Upanishad, noting this external orientation, says that a wise man turned the mind inward and there discovered the Self.

Ramana here is suggesting that we do the same. But how, exactly, are we to accomplish this redirection?

Vedanta teaches discrimination of the Self from the not-Self (*atma* from *anatma*). Beginning with the grossest and most stubborn misidentification, the body, we are led to increasingly subtle misidentifications until we arrive at the intellect, called the *buddhi*. In each instance, the agreement-and-difference logic, *anvaya/vyatireka*, is applied. When this object or thought or feeling is here, I am here; when this object or thought or feeling is not here, I am still here. So, I am independent of all of these external things, which are really mental images.

The intellect, however, appears to be the very source of this discrimination and identical with awareness. We take the *buddhi* to be the subject, the Self. It is an understandable assumption, for the light of awareness shines in the intellect and illumines all the other objects. The intellect is the most subtle matter, called *sattva*, and like a spotless mirror, it has the capacity to reflect awareness so clearly that it is difficult to distinguish the mirror from the light it reflects.

But the intellect is not the Self; it is not me. When I am in deep sleep, it is resolved into consciousness and no longer reflects anything. The intellect is gone then, but I continue to exist. So, it is not essential to me. The intellect, too, is an object: it, too, can be externalized and negated.

When, in the waking state, I am able to make this discrimination and recognize that I am not the intellect, what is left for me to identify with? Who am I then? I must be the light reflected in the intellect: awareness itself.

Now, if all the objects external to awareness can be objectified by me, the individual, then the same must be true of *Ishwara*, the total. If I cannot be any object of which I am aware, then neither can *Ishwara*. What is left for me as my core identity is the same as that which is the core identity of *Ishwara*: awareness. And awareness cannot be divided, as existence cannot be divided. To have the vision of *Ishwara* is to recognize my Self.

Turning the mind inward means negating all the external objects with which I habitually identify until the Self alone remains. There, in that undivided, unobjectifiable awareness, *Ishwara* is me and I am *Ishwara*. There is no second thing: *advaita*.

Verse 23

The body does not say "I."
No one says "I" did not exist in deep sleep.
When the "I" rises, all rise.
Find out with keen intellect, whence this "I"?

The default position for the "I" thought is "I am the body." So unquestioning is our identification with the physical form that countless billions of hard-earned dollars are spent each year on diet and exercise programs designed to make the body more attractive. The thought modification, "I am fat," generates all manner of action on the part of one who believes that he is defined by the weight and shape of his flesh.

But Ramana begins this verse with the observation that the body never says "I." The body, in fact, never says anything: it is a mute composition of inert elements. It can no more say "I" than can the table or the doormat.

Ramana then shifts our focus to deep sleep and points out that no one says he ceased to exist while in deep sleep. Why is this an important observation? Because in deep sleep, the "I" thought is completely absent. This process of identification with objects that is the activity of the "I" thought comes to an end. Yet, I do not prepare for bed at night in the belief that I will cease to exist in deep sleep, when the "I" thought is not present.

Ramana wants us to consider this fact carefully. In the light of logic, if I continue to exist without the "I" thought, then the "I" thought is not essential to my being: I am not the "I" thought. Then what is this mysterious "I" thought that comes and goes and seems to take me along with it whenever it arises?

We are counseled to use our mind to look carefully into the origin of this "I" thought. Ramana observes that it is only when the "I" thought arises that all other objects arise. In deep sleep, when the "I" thought is absent, objects are also absent. When we awake and the "I" thought returns, the world of objects returns. Applying our logic again, we can conclude that when the "I" thought is here, the world of objects is here; when the "I" thought is not here, the world of objects is not here. Therefore, the "I" thought and the world of objects are mutually dependent: one cannot appear without the other.

What is the "I" thought that is synonymous with my awareness of the world of objects? And where does it go in deep sleep? And where does it come from when I awake? Ramana begins to examine these questions in the following verses.

Verse 24

The body is insentient.
The Self does not rise. Within the body's limit, an "I" rises
Between the body and Self. It is named "ego,"
"Knot of matter and spirit," "bondage," "subtle body" and "mind."

The "I" thought comes and goes. Where does it come from? It cannot come from the body, for the body has no awareness: it makes no comment upon its being. In Vedanta, it is called *annamaya kosha* – the food sheath. It is made of inert matter, feeds on food, decomposes into food. It is not the source of the "I" thought, for the body doesn't think.

Can the "I" thought arise in the Self, that is, in awareness? The Self does not come and go, so it cannot be synonymous with the "I" thought. The Self also never changes, so the "I" thought cannot be a property of the Self, for the "I" thought is ever an actor, moving through the changing experiences with which it successively identifies.

So, if neither the body nor the Self gives rise to the "I" thought, what does? Ramana wants us to be aware that he is here trying to assign a name and origin to something that has no real being. It is like trying to look into the nature of the snake in the rope. There is no snake; only ignorance of the rope. There is no ego; only ignorance of the Self.

Yet, we experience the "I" thought, so it has at least a provisional existence, which is to say, it is *mithya* – totally dependent on that which is real. Ramana describes the "I" thought as something that appears to arise in the proximity of the body and the Self and appears to tie them together. Although it is neither, it borrows aspects of the body and the Self from which it creates its phantom being. It does this by the process mentioned before: mutual superimposition.

An analogy may be helpful. When our face is reflected in a mirror, the reflection is not really our face; neither is it purely the mirror. The image in the mirror has qualities of both our face and the substance from which the mirror is made. But the reflection has no reality in itself. The "I" thought borrows from the nature of the Self (awareness) and the body (physical substance and sense organs). It then imposes one upon the other, attributing awareness to the body and the body to awareness. In this manner, the "I" thought appears to exist. But the "I" thought has no reality in itself.

The purpose of Vedanta is to discriminate the "I" thought from awareness and the objects it wrongly identifies with awareness. This is done by realizing the truth of the sentences of the Upanishads and other source texts of Vedanta. These words correctly point us to awareness, which is what we are, and end the superimposition of our nature on objects. They expose mutual superimposition and do away with it, thus doing away with the "I" thought.

Ramana gives a list of names for the "I" thought so that we can consider it from several angles and not be misled when it shifts its emphasis in the act of mutual superimposition. The first name is "ego," by which we are to understand the "I" thought as an actor, always trying to acquire something to complete itself. The second is "knot of matter and spirit," which signifies the superimposition of awareness on the body, and the body on awareness, attributing the character of the one to the other and vice versa. The third one is "bondage," which causes us to think that we own things and are tied to them, and thus tied to the world of objects. The fourth is "subtle body," which stands for the composite nature of the "I" thought. It is subtle, in that it cannot be perceived by the gross sense instruments; and it is a body, for it experiences birth and death, like all bodies: the changing "I" thoughts are forever coming into existence and perishing shortly thereafter. And the last name on the list is "mind," for the "I" thought takes the reflection of awareness in the mind for the Self, and thus confuses the contents of the mind with that which illumines the mind, regardless of content.

Verse 25

Born of forms, rooted in forms,
Feeding on forms, ever changing its forms,
Itself formless, this ego-ghost
Takes to its heels on inquiry.

The "I" thought in Sanskrit is called *ahankara*. The translation into "I" thought is not entirely accurate. The first two syllables stand for "I" and the *"kara"* suffix is attached to a word to indicate its capacity to make or produce. A more exact rendering would be "I maker." Ramana told us in the previous verse that the "I maker" is composed of elements borrowed from the body and the Self.

From the Self, it borrows its sense of existence/awareness, which is the "I am." From the body or any other mental or physical object, it borrows the various predicates it attaches to the "I am," such as "I am fat, smart, stupid, happy, sad, rich, poor, hungry, etc." The "I" thought has no intrinsic identity: it is a composite, and like all composites, it is subject to decomposition. When it decomposes, that is, when discrimination separates the Self from the predicates attached to it, the "I" thought falls apart. It loses its illusory being, much like the snake disappears when its superimposition upon the rope becomes known.

Ramana says the "I" thought arises with forms. A form – *rupa* – is a mental image to which we give a name. We may say, "The table exists," which means, the table thought appearing in my mind exists, but the table thought is a form in awareness, and the table, as an object, has no existence in itself. Its appearance is a composite of infinitely reducible forms – wood, cellulose, molecules, atoms, particles, etc. – that we signify by a word, and none of those forms exists in themselves. In fact, when we look at the table, we do not see existence; we see form. Existence is superimposed upon the form. Thus, we attribute existence to names that are infinitely divisible forms.

The "I" thought attaches itself to forms on which it superimposes existence/awareness. The chief of these forms is the body, but the variety of possible forms is endless. When we examine these forms, we realize that they come and go and cannot possibly be the Self that is present before they arise and that remains after they have departed. The existence we attribute to these forms is our own existence, which is unattached to any form.

Ramana calls the ego a ghost. A ghost has no substance. It haunts the world of substances, hungry to assume a living form but unable to do so. Ghosts frighten us because we fear that we might become one when the body dies. But the fact is, we have already become ghosts to the extent that we identify with the "I" thought. The ego, like the ghost, is a shadow with no life of its own. It haunts us day and night and only goes away during deep sleep or when we become established in the knowledge of the Self.

If we look into its nature, Ramana says, the ego ghost will vanish, never to return. If we discriminate the composite nature of the "I" thought and recognize that we are that which can never be a composite, for we are whole and complete and unattached to all that comes and goes, then the "I maker" will cease its ghostly activity and we will rest in the changeless Self.

Verse 26

On the rising of the ego, everything rises.
With its subsidence, all subside.
The ego is therefore all.
Tracking it is the way to victory over everything.

The Self has no problems, which means I have no problems. So why do I often feel beset by difficulties? Why do I feel "the world is too much with us," as the poet laments? Because the world arises when the "I" thought arises, and I compound my identity with the changing objects the senses perceive and the mind cognizes. And as the objects, including all thoughts and feelings, have no stability, I believe I have no stability. Even whatever happiness I may enjoy, I attribute to objects, so it is slipping away from me even as I am experiencing it.

After a day of attaching myself to one thing after another and finding no lasting satisfaction, I long for sleep; that is, I want to obliterate the world by extinguishing my "I" thought. If I really believed that my existence and my "I" thought were one and the same, sleep would terrify me. On the contrary, I look forward to sleep with intense pleasure. I sometimes can't wait to fall into the "dreamless," as we call it. I want to end all the identifications that keep me running on the wheel of *samsara* like a hamster in a cage.

When I do fall into deep sleep, the waking world and the dream world dissolve. The "I" thought is no longer present and, with its disappearance, the world of objects also disappears. And the absence of the "I" thought and the world feels wonderful. We are having an experience of non-duality, even if we lack the knowledge of non-duality. And we don't want our deep sleep to be disturbed.

But each day, we awake. The "I" thought returns and the

world of objects, which are the field of experience for the "I" thought, comes with it. Ramana invites us to use our logic of *anvaya-vyatireka* – agreement and difference – to establish the mutual dependence of the ego and the world: when the ego is there, the world is there; when the ego is not there, the world is not there. Therefore, the ego and the world arise and subside together.

But Ramana's focus is always on the "I" thought, the ego. He tells us that if we follow the "I" thought to its source, we need not concern ourselves with the world, for the world will dissolve when the "I" thought dissolves. This does not mean that objects will no longer be perceived by our senses or the mind will cease to operate. It means that we will no longer compound our identity with objects that come and go. We will see that objects depend on awareness for their existence: the pot cannot exist without the clay. In fact, the pot is the clay. And the ego, the "I" thought, has no being apart from awareness, which is me.

Verse 27

The "I" does not rise in the real state.
Search for the source of "I" dissolves it.
How else can one attain
The supreme state of one's own Self?

If you destroy the cause, you eliminate the effect. Ramana has been urging us in these verses to investigate the cause of the "I" thought. This cause is ignorance of the Self. If I know I am limitless existence/awareness, I will not identify with a body or a feeling or a thought. And it is only such identification that constitutes the "I" thought. When it ceases, the "I" thought dissolves. What is left is what is always here: the pure "I" with no attachments.

Ramana refers to the "real state" in which the "I" thought cannot arise. He has told us previously that the Self does not say "I," for there is only the Self, and "I" implies "you" and "it." The ego brings the world with it and gives rise to duality. But duality is *mithya*: when "I" see "you," awareness appears as two things. But awareness cannot be divided, just as existence cannot be divided. Can awareness be discontinuous? Can it blink on and off, or fall into periods of unawareness? Is there some space between you and me where awareness does not exist? And can existence give way to non-existence, so that objects can be separated and individuated by intervals of non-existence? Your body is not my body, and your thoughts are not my thoughts, but your awareness is my awareness. It cannot be otherwise.

What is seen or experienced in the empirical world is not ultimately different from the seer. On the highest level – *paramarthika* – the "I" thought does not arise because there is no subject/object differentiation. There is no break in existence/

awareness. There is really no seer because there is nothing to be seen. Awareness does not know itself, as though it were objectified: it is and it is all that is.

Verse 28

Discover the real source of the ego by exploring within,
With keen intellect, by regulating breath, speech and mind
As one would do to recover a thing
Which has fallen into a deep well.

Ramana has been urging us to track the "I" thought to its source. In this verse, he becomes more specific about how to go about this investigation. The advice to employ "keen intellect" has been offered previously, but now we are told that to sharpen our intellect for this inquiry we should pay attention to the breath, speech and mind.

One of the steps listed in the Yoga Sutras as preliminary to meditation is *pranayama*, generally translated as control of the breath. But prana stands for the animating force that enlivens the body and operates its physiological systems. It is connected to the breath, however, and can be deliberately affected by exercises that regulate our breathing in various ways. We know that when we are agitated, our breathing becomes short and rapid; when we are calm, our breathing is slow and steady. We cannot effectively discriminate the Self from the shifting "I" thoughts unless our mind is quiet and clear.

The reflection of awareness in the mind has been likened to the reflection of the sun in a bucket of water. If the water is muddy, it will give only a dim reflection; if it is moving, the reflection will be broken up; if it is still, the reflection will be true to the reflected source. To realize that the mind is not the source of consciousness, but merely a reflecting medium, requires clarity and stillness in the intellect. This can be achieved, in some measure, by controlling the breath. Ramana recommends that we make use of this help.

We are also counseled to regulate speech. The advantage

of doing so should be obvious. How many difficulties and contentions arise from unguarded speech? A thought arises; we lay claim to it; it arouses our emotions; we give voice to it. We then become mired in all the consequences of having spoken. To what end? Excitement and argument.

The chief value of what is called the *sanatana dharma*, which corresponds in the West to what we call the universal natural law, is non-injury – *ahimsa*. And one of the cardinal rules for non-injury is *vak tapas* – control of one's speech. We are advised not to say anything unless it meets three criteria: it must be true; it must be beneficial; it must be pleasing (*satyam, hitam, priyam*).

If there is any doubt about the veracity of a statement, don't make it. Why spread dubious information? If no one is helped by a statement, what value can it have? And if what is said is harsh and unpleasant, it will only produce revulsion and ill-feeling. We can spare ourselves and others a great deal of misery by control of speech. Imagine how political discourse could be improved were *vak tapas* observed? But the main advantage in observing it for one engaged in Self-inquiry is that it conduces to a quiet mind in which the reflection of awareness can be discerned more clearly.

Ramana also recommends control of the mind. Vedanta makes a distinction between mind and intellect. The former has largely to do with forming impressions of objects and the emotions these objects evoke; the intellect has to do with the "I" thought, that is, with the ego and its activities of deciding and doing. When the mind is churning in a sea of objects and emotions, the intellect becomes preoccupied with all that the mind presents for its consideration. What is called "multi-tasking" is really the intellect trying to keep up with the frantic pace of runaway mental activity. Unless the mind is taken in hand, it will keep the intellect in a perpetual state of reaction and won't allow it to turn its attention to the awareness whose illumination it enjoys.

So Ramana in this verse offers practical advice. None of these recommendations will, in themselves, lead to Self-realization, for the Self is already realized. No action is needed to achieve it, for it cannot and need not be achieved. The point of calming the breath, controlling the speech and settling the mind is to allow the intellect to turn away from objects and turn to its source: awareness, which is me.

Ramana also describes an attitude to be adopted in pursuing these recommendations: we should be determined, like one intent upon recovering something that has fallen into a deep well. Retrieving an object from a deep well presents obvious difficulties: the well bottom is dark and the object is covered by water. Many attempts will probably be required, such as repeated lowerings of a bucket until the object is drawn up. Patience, perseverance and one-pointed attention are needed.

The Self, however, need not be recovered, for it has never been lost. What Ramana wants to convey is that the confusion of the Self with objects, which constitutes the "I" thought, is stubborn and habitual, reinforced by countless lifetimes. It will not disappear until the intellect has sufficient clarity to recognize the truth of the sentences of Vedanta. And such clarity can be aided by deliberate exercises to eliminate distractions.

Verse 29

To enquire silently and deeply as to the source of the mind,
The "I," alone is Self-enquiry.
Ideas like, "I am that" or "I am not this"
Are but aids.

The misunderstanding of the nature of Self-inquiry – *atma vichara* – has led some devotees to believe that an independent probing of the mind with the intent of discovering the "true I" is the path Ramana urged us to follow. In this verse, we are told to inquire "silently and deeply" into the source of the "I" thought. This does not mean that we can, on our own, clear up our habitual confusion about who we are.

Inquiry in Vedanta means listening – *sravana*. To what do we listen? We listen to the teacher who unfolds the meaning of the Upanishads and other texts that tell us who we are. If we rely on our own understanding, we will never come to this knowledge. It is as though we have fallen into a pit too deep for us to climb out of on our own. We need a hand. The teacher and the text are that hand. If we don't take it, we will remain in the pit, no matter how many beautiful thoughts we generate about what it might be like to be free of the pit.

To inquire "silently" does not simply mean to stop talking and think quietly. It means clearing the mind of obstructions so that we can listen to the teaching. We have to tell our mind, that is, our own thoughts, to go and sit in the corner for a while. Then, the intellect can hear without hindrance the sentences of the Upanishads and other texts that reveal our true nature. This silence must also be deep, that is, firmly held. A superficial and fleeting silence will not allow the intellect to become established in the knowledge of its own source. It will be drawn away from listening into the recurring chatter of the mind.

We might use techniques such as *neti, neti* – not this, not this – to negate the "I" thoughts that identify us with physical and mental objects. And we can contemplate statements such as *so'ham* – I am that, with "that" meaning *Brahman*. These will help us to recognize who we are. They bring us closer to conforming knowledge to reality, but the "I" thought is still present: there is still subject/object duality between the "I" and what it is and is not. When one reaches the source of the "I," Ramana says, these aids are no longer necessary. Then, we no longer have to define who we are and are not: we simply rest in limitless awareness, which cannot be defined.

Versse 30

The ego falls, crestfallen, when one enquires,
"Who am I?" and enters the heart.
Then, another "I-I," throbs unceasingly, by itself.
It is not the ego, but the Self itself, the whole.

To ask the question, "Who am I?" is to admit that the "I" thought is not me. If I were satisfied with the various identities supplied by the mind's shifting attachments, I would not ask the question. So, the prerequisite for this inquiry into the ego is the recognition that the "I" thought is just that: a thought. Like all thoughts, it is seen, which means it is an object and not the subject.

Unlike other objects, however, the "I" thought has a relative permanence which gives us the impression that it is our fixed identity. Other objects come and go quickly and we do not think we are anything that we perceive. Yet, we think we are the "I" thought because it has its source in the awareness that lights up all the objects we know, including the "I" thought. We confuse the "I" thought with existence/awareness. This is what is called superimposition.

Every perception and thought are related to me as existence/awareness. If I say, "That is a table," what is implied in the statement is, "I am aware of a form appearing in my mind which I call 'table'." All experience of external and internal objects is prefaced with "I am." This "I am" is the Self, which is the subject of Vedanta. The teaching methods used in Self-inquiry are intended to separate the Self from the not-Self; the "I am" from the "I am this" and "I am that."

All that is added to existence/awareness is name and form. The predicates that follow the statement "I am" are all *mithya*: they have no reality independent of the Self. They are like the pot in the clay or the snake in the rope. They are like the pot in the clay because all mental images appear in awareness and are nothing but awareness. They are like the snake in the rope because their apparent existence as independent entities is not real. When seen for what they are, they disappear, like the snake in the rope.

Ramana says that if we inquire deeply and persistently into the nature of the ego, it will fall away, for it has no substance. In fact, it is constantly falling away, as one notion of who we are is always being negated and replaced by a succeeding notion. Inquiry into the ego can bring this mad parade of "I" thoughts to a halt. Then, Ramana says, we will enter the heart, which stands for the Self. There, the "I-I" is known as the unchanging Self. We stop attaching predicates to the "I am" and rest in existence/ awareness, whole and complete.

Verse 31

Who can understand the state of the one
Who has dissolved the ego and is abiding, always, in the Self?
For him, the Self alone is.
What remains for him to do?

When we stop confusing the unchanging "I" with thoughts and emotions that come and go, the ego falls away. It is merely a product of this confusion, called superimposition. It is the "knot of the heart" that ties the "I" to the "I" thoughts. It creates a hybrid persona, made up of existence/awareness and names and forms, but it posits the names and forms as having a unique and independent existence. In this way, it reverses the true position in which names and forms are *mithya* – entirely dependent on the one and only existence/awareness outside of which there is nothing: no second thing – *advaita*. When one unties this knot, the ego dissolves. Leaning on the analogy a bit further, we can say that the ego has no more independent being than the knot. The "I" thought depends on the "I" just as the knot depends on the rope. There is no "I" thought without the "I" and there is no knot without the rope. But the "I" exists without the "I" thought and the rope exists without the knot.

When the ego dissolves, we no longer see our Self as tied to the objects we perceive or imagine. We give up having to become something by acquiring this and discarding that. The incessant composition and editing of body and personality comes to an end: no more body sculpting, self-help books, therapies, get-rich-quick seminars, Botox treatments; no more drugs, alcohol, dogmatism or mysticism. When we jump off the wheel of *samsara,* we stop chasing happiness in objects and experiences. And this will make us radical non-conformists; that is, content.

Ramana asks how one who is still laboring in the world under the spell of the ego can understand one who has dissolved the ego? The ego-identified person needs to do things and have things to be happy, or so he believes. The one who has dissolved the ego needs nothing, not even worldly happiness, which is bound to experiences and, therefore, transient. The one who has dissolved the ego acts according to his circumstances and the duties of his state in life. But there is nothing he has to do to be pleased with his Self. If he acts, he does so freely and not because he hopes to gain something he believes essential to his happiness.

Verse 32

The scriptures assert "That you are."
Without enquiring and reaching the Self which always shines
And abiding as that, to discuss again, endlessly,
Is only due to the weakness of the mind.

The "I" thought can become attached to anything, even to Self-inquiry. The purpose of Self-inquiry is to remove the ignorance that obscures our true nature and confuses it with objects that have no permanence or inherent joy. Strange as it may seem, losing sight of the purpose of Self-inquiry and making the process an end in itself is possible.

Vedanta is not a creed or religious practice. It is called a "means of knowledge" – a *pramana*. The principal thing to be borne in mind concerning a means is that it is to be discarded once the end is achieved. The means of knowledge Vedanta provides are the *mahavakyas*, the great sentences that tell us who we are. Swami Dayananda used to say that Vedanta offers us a word picture of the Self.

The most often quoted *mahavakya* is "That you are," which Ramana cites in the first line of the above verse. He says that having heard this truth, one should realize it by immersing oneself in the proper inquiry. But there are those who rather choose to make it a subject of discussion: they want to debate, write papers, speculate and opine, as though the *mahavakya* were an academic proposition subject to their interpretation.

One can read many books about Vedanta written by scholars of Sanskrit and the Upanishads and still be mired in ignorance. Knowledge of Vedanta can become just another "I" thought; indeed, it is a very seductive one, for it substitutes the acquisition of learning for the shedding of ignorance. The ego is only too happy to burnish its résumé with an accumulation of knowledge. The image of a donkey with books on its back is sometimes used to illustrate the pointlessness of an erudition that does not lead to *moksha* – liberation from the ego.

Ramana warns us of losing sight of the goal of Self-inquiry and making it subservient to the ego, rather than its destroyer. "That you are" equates the individual with the total, the *jiva* with *Ishwara*. It is a sentence that conforms the mind to reality. For an *uttama adhikari* – the most highly qualified person – hearing it once is enough.

Ramana was an *uttama adhikari*, for his mind had been purified by years of deep meditation. Most of us are not in that position. We hear the *mahavakya* and need to have it explained to us by a qualified teacher, perhaps again and again, for we have many "I" thoughts stirring up great clouds of dust in our minds and we cannot see clearly until the dust settles.

Ramana cautions us to keep the goal of Self-inquiry always before us, lest we lose sight of the very purpose of Vedanta, which is to know who we are, not to amass more knowledge about yet another subject.

Versse 33

Statements like, "I do not know my Self"
Or "I know my Self" are matter for laughter.
Are there two selves, the seer and the seen?
The experience of all is that the Self is one.

Having just cautioned us about the danger of making the process of Self-inquiry an end in itself, Ramana tells us what can happen when we take the Self to be an object like other objects. The very phrase, "Self-knowledge" implies that there are two things present: the knower and that which is to be known. Vedanta has to use language that is intrinsically dualistic, which is why we need a teacher capable of making words that normally describe limitation point to that which is limitless.

Who is the knower? He is that which is separate from the object to be known. If I want to know Sanskrit, I may study the subject and acquire a mastery of it with no alteration in the person I consider myself to be. I have simply added, "knower of Sanskrit" to my collection of "I" thoughts. Self-knowledge is not like this. I can never add, "knower of the Self" to my "I" thoughts.

In a previous verse, Ramana said that we can only know God, the absolute, by "becoming food" for Him. That is, the ego must be offered to the sacrificial fire, like a piece of camphor that burns and leaves no residue. So long as we maintain a "knower" of the Self, we do not and cannot know the Self.

There is much talk in Western spiritual circles about "enlightenment" and there are many teachers and practices that promise to make you enlightened. But *you* can never become enlightened, for "you" – the knower – are the very thing that has to be given up for the Self to be realized. This is what is meant by enlightenment.

In the Katha Upanishad, the teacher is Death, personified as the god Yama. Like Nachiketas, the young boy who bravely approaches Yama, we must be willing to die – to give up all the "I" thoughts to which the ego clings as though to life itself – for Self-knowledge. So long as the "I" thoughts persist, we will remain in ignorance. When the Self is known, the "I" thoughts disappear. We only see the snake when we don't know the rope.

To say that I know or do not know the Self is to treat the Self as though it were something that can be gained, like other sorts of knowledge. But the Self is already and always present. It cannot be gained. If it could be gained, it could also be lost, for it would be subject to time, which is change. We already know the Self, for we know that we are and that we are conscious; we simply confuse our conscious being with objects that appear in our awareness; we mistake the not-Self for the Self. And the knower, as "I" thought, is the not-Self. It has to go if our confusion is to be cleared up.

Verse 34

Instead of firmly abiding in the heart
In one's own, true state,
To quarrel "real" or "unreal," with "form" or "formless,"
"Many" or "one" is to be blinded by illusion.

Ramana continues his warning about becoming immersed in argument and discussion concerning the nature of the Self. The topic is prolonged because erudition and triumph in controversy can be powerful inducements to those who are inclined to serious inquiry. Intellectual accomplishment offers a certain satisfaction: it is measurable and within the grasp of the ego.

One may come to Vedanta with a burning desire for liberation: to be free from the "I" thoughts that drive us to the futile pursuit of a happiness that we superimpose on objects and then run after, like a dog chasing its tail. But we may come to make the knowledge of Vedanta – Sanskrit, scripture, logic, commentaries – the thing that we chase, as we chase other objects in *samsara* – the world of becoming. But because we want to become an authority in Vedanta, we can believe that we are pursuing Self-knowledge, when we are only pursuing knowledge about the tools used in Self-inquiry. We are then like a builder who is forever arranging and adding to his toolbox but who never builds anything.

Speculation and controversy are the domain of the pundit. The *mahavakya* gives direct knowledge, which puts an end to punditry. Teaching may be needed, and the teacher may indeed be learned, but the means of knowledge is the scripture, not auxiliary subjects that may or may not help one to see clearly the truth that is being spoken.

Verse 35

Self-abidance alone is a miracle.
The other miracles are like dreams which last till waking.
Can those firmly rooted in the real
Relapse into illusion?

The word "miracle" in this verse comes from a Sanskrit word –
siddhi – which has several levels of meaning, from the mundane
to the mystical. It generally signifies accomplishment, and in
this respect, can stand for anything one brings about through
action. But it also means that which is brought about through
sadhana – spiritual practices. In the Yoga literature, a *siddhi* is an
extraordinary power, such as psychic ability, acquired through
intense austerity or special techniques.

A discussion of *siddhi* is not relevant to this commentary.
Ramana has introduced the topic to illustrate that actions that
amaze us, that we may call miraculous, impress us only so long
as we do not know the Self. If this is so, what can be said about
ordinary actions and their results?

Every action has as its aim the creation, modification,
attainment or refinement of something: it effects a change and
is therefore bound by time. Anything bound by time comes
and goes and is not real as Vedanta defines reality: that which
cannot be negated in past, present or future.

So long as we project our Self onto objects, we will chase
objects trying to recapture the Self, for we love what we truly
are and our desire is to rest in our own nature. When St.
Augustine made his famous declaration to God: "Our hearts
were made for Thee, and cannot rest until they rest in Thee," he
was expressing, in the idiom of Christianity, the fundamental
truth of the human condition. The Self, our timeless being, is
what we want and what we seek in all of our actions. It is the

only place where we can rest.

Ramana calls Self-abidance the real miracle: that is, the uniquely great accomplishment. But it is not an accomplishment in the sense that something that did not exist previously is produced by an action or series of actions. It is the recognition that we are all that we desire, all that we know, all that we do. We cannot gain anything, nor lose anything. Gain and loss, the results of action, occur only on the empirical level. Even the greatest perceived miracle is nothing other than consciousness and, as such, is not essentially different from any other thing we experience in this world.

To know that we are existence/awareness; that we are what we love and seek in objects is the supreme *siddhi*. Once we know this, Ramana asks, is there any possibility of falling back into the illusion that our happiness lies outside of us, in objects and powers to be attained by action and lost in time?

Verse 36

So long as we have the idea that the body is the Self,
The thought that one is the Self is helpful for being That.
But when one is That, it is as futile as a man repeating,
"I am a man," "I am a man."

Knowledge has a permanence that experience lacks. We can observe the mental state of happiness being succeeded by the mental state of sadness, for mental states change without ceasing, as do perceptions of objects that come and go through the sense organs. But once we know something, that knowledge becomes established. We can return to it whenever we have need of it and it will be there in its permanent form.

The early Greeks observed that mathematical truths are timeless, and from this fact they inferred that there must be a domain of timeless truth: philosophy then took birth in the West. When we discover that $2 + 2 = 4$, we have recognized a truth that cannot be negated at any time and that is always available to us. But before we have learned this simple bit of arithmetic, we may have to revert to it for a time until it becomes settled knowledge. We may have to do some homework.

Ramana tells us that as long as we think we are a composition of "I" thoughts rather than pure awareness, we may have to remind ourselves of the truths put forth in the *mahavakya*. The most persistent "I" thought is "I am the body." So long as it lasts it will have to be countered with the thought, "I am that" – with "that" meaning limitless existence and knowledge. And this is why we must be committed to constant Self-inquiry – *atma vichara*.

But once we realize that we are, indeed, the Self and not the body, we no longer have to contemplate the equation, "I am that." Just as when we learn that $2 + 2 = 4$, we need not keep repeating it, for the knowledge cannot be forgotten or contradicted. When we recognize the "I" to be limitless existence/awareness, we need not continue to remind ourselves of the fact, lest we lose sight of it. But before the knowledge of the Self becomes firm, Ramana says, it is useful to continue to make the discrimination that the body is in awareness, not awareness in the body.

Sometimes, in our eagerness for Self-knowledge, we will ask the teacher, "How long must I do this inquiry before I am liberated?" The answer can only be, "As long as it takes." It is not as though something will be accomplished in time, as is the case with actions needed to bring into being that which was not previously present. The Self is always present. But the mind is not always established in the knowledge of the Self. It sometimes knows, and sometimes forgets. Time is needed, not to realize the Self, but to acquire steadiness in the knowledge of the Self, which is called *nishta*.

Verse 37

The theories such as duality in sadhana and advaita
On Realization are not true.
The tenth man was present not only when he was found,
But also during the search with loving concern.

We think we are ignorant and must adopt certain practices to attain knowledge. There are a great many teachers and belief systems that encourage us to pursue some course of action that promises Realization or Enlightenment as the result of a prolonged and arduous regimen, and perhaps a bit of money. All such practices are rooted in the notion that the Self is an experience to be had in time.

All throughout these verses, Ramana has been telling us that the Self is not realized by action of any sort, but by knowledge. Our problem is ignorance, not inexperience. The quest for enlightenment is generally presented as a striving for an ultimate experience that will establish us in a state of permanent bliss. But no state, blissful or miserable, can be permanent, for it is a condition of the mind or body, both of which are time-bound: they come and go and are not real as Vedanta defines reality – that which cannot be negated in past, present or future.

Ramana tells us in this verse that the idea that duality is overcome and realization occurs in time as the result of *sadhana* – some form of spiritual practice – is seen to be false when one recognizes the Self, for the Self was never absent and did not need to be attained. To illustrate this, Ramana refers to the story of the Tenth Man, which students of Vedanta will hear again and again from teachers and texts.

The story is that a group of ten boys undertake a pilgrimage and, at a certain point, must swim across a fast-moving river. When they arrive on the opposite shore, their leader does a head-count to make certain they all crossed successfully. He counts only nine boys. Distressed, he counts again and again, then announces tearfully to the group that one of their number perished in the river. The group is sitting on the riverbank, crying and lamenting, when a woodcutter observes them and approaches to ask why they are so upset. "We were ten, and now we are only nine. One of us drowned trying to cross the river!" the leader tells him.

The woodcutter smiles and tells the leader that he has found the tenth man and that he is well and safe. The leader is relieved but skeptical, "Where is he?" he asks. "I will show him to you," the woodcutter says, and asks the leader to count the boys one more time. When the leader reaches nine, as he has many times previously, the woodcutter points to the leader and says, "Ten! You are the tenth man!" The leader forgot to count himself.

Now, the point of the story is that the tenth man was not found by the woodcutter: he was always present. All the counting by the leader and the mourning for the absent comrade were the result, not of any real loss or absence, but of ignorance of an ever-present fact. The Self is the tenth man. We search for the Self in many places, that is, in many experiences, hoping to realize who we are as an event in time. But we are already the Self. We cannot and need not be brought into being by any *sadhana* or experience.

When we try to realize the Self through actions, we are like the leader counting to nine and wondering where the tenth man is when *we are the tenth man*. And as soon as we are told we are the tenth man, we recognize it as the truth. We no longer believe there was ever a time when the tenth man did not exist.

But Ramana pays respect to the search carried out with "loving concern," for it is our devotion to the truth that prepares our mind to receive knowledge. Vedanta is sometimes faulted for being dry or intellectual, but the inquiry needed to discover the existent truth can only be sustained by a heart filled with faith and love. To revert to our analogy, the tenth man is sought because the tenth man is dear to his friends. If Vedanta is pursued as a merely intellectual exercise, it may lead to a certain expertise in Sanskrit and source texts, but it will not lead to liberation from ignorance. Only the desire for truth, sustained by love, will free us.

Verse 38

If one feels one is the doer, one must reap the fruits of his action.
If one enquires, "Who is the doer?"
And enters the heart, the doership idea will end.
Triple karma is destroyed. This indeed is liberation.

Not knowing who we are, we define ourselves by our actions. We become, first and foremost, a doer. The initial question we usually ask a new acquaintance is, "So, what do you do?" We then identify the person by his modes of action: what he does to make money; what he does for exercise, recreation, etc.

Ramana says that so long as we identify ourselves and others with the doer, we are bound by action. This means that we must continue to generate the results of actions and receive their consequences. This process is called karma. Karma, in Western usage, generally has a negative connotation: it is an exotic word for the more homely expression, "comeuppance." Karma is most often used to designate a deserved punishment. There can be "good" karma, too, but we prefer to take personal credit for good things rather than assign them to an impersonal process of cosmic justice.

What drives us to act? We are unhappy. We feel incomplete, inadequate. "If I do this, I will feel better," or so we believe. We commit ourselves to some course of action in the hope that it will alleviate the sense that something is missing in our lives. But what is missing is the knowledge of who we are: actionless, timeless, utterly complete existence/awareness.

Whenever we do something, we act in time and we will receive a time-bound result. As has been observed frequently in this commentary, anything time-bound will come and go. We do not come and go. Were we time-bound we would cease to exist when the action or its result ceased to exist. It should be obvious that we cannot be the actor or his actions, but so ingrained is our habit of identifying with the body and its organs of action that it seems natural to think we are the doer.

Ramana wants us to ask the simple question: "Who is the doer?" Awareness cannot be the doer, for it has no organs of action. It is the light by which all things are known, including actions, but it does not act. Neither does it say "I," for it is not separate from "you" or "it." The Self is everything and there is no second thing: *advaita*. The Self cannot say, "I do this." Who says it?

The intellect decides what to do and then identifies itself with the doer of the action, the "I" thought that is called the *ahankara* – the "I" maker. But the intellect is part of the subtle body and is, in itself, inert. Thoughts cannot know themselves or generate other thoughts: only consciousness – the aware being – can light up the contents of the intellect. So, the *ahankara* – the shifting "I" thought, is not really a doer. When it says, "I do this," it is merely presenting a thought to awareness that awareness lights up. Without awareness there is no thought, including the thought of being a doer.

There is a wonderful simile in Vedanta that likens awareness to a water tank in a field. When the spigot of the tank is opened, the water will flow into the field and take its shape. But water, in itself, has no shape. And when it follows the channels into the field, it does not change its nature. It remains shapeless water seemingly in the shape of the field. Just so, awareness appears to assume the shape of the thought it illumines, but it remains changeless awareness. The thought, "I am the doer" is awareness appearing as that particular thought. But the thought, being time-bound, will be replaced by another thought, and so on, while awareness can never be replaced by anything. It remains, complete and actionless, at all times and through all the changes the body/mind undergoes.

Once we recognize that we are not the "I" thought that

identifies with bodily actions and that we need do nothing to be complete, the impetus for action comes to an end. We will continue to do what we must so long as the body lasts, for the results of past actions have already been set in motion and cannot be stopped, much like an arrow released from the bow cannot be stopped in mid-flight. But we will no longer accumulate karma by doing things in the hope that they will bring us the fruits of happiness. And, according to the scriptures, we will also be freed from the results of whatever karma has been stored up but not yet experienced. The reasoning is that karma requires a doer, an "I" thought to which it must be attached; when the "I" thought of "I am the doer" is not there, karma has no place to go, no vehicle. This release from karma, Ramana says, is true freedom – *moksha*.

Verse 39

Thoughts of liberation are only so long as one thinks one is bound.
One attains the eternally liberated "I" by the enquiry,
"For whom is the bondage?"
Thereafter, how can thought of freedom and bondage arise?

Were one who practices some discipline of Eastern spirituality to be asked, "Why are you doing these things?" his likely answer would be, "To become enlightened." A simpler and more direct answer would be, "To become happy."

Enlightenment is generally understood as a state in which one is happy all the time. And since we all want to be happy all the time, it is only natural that any practice or belief or devotion that promises a state of uninterrupted bliss should acquire a following.

The person who wants to be happy is the unhappy person. Unhappiness comes from not being pleased with who we think we are. We don't like our face or figure; we think we are not smart enough or rich enough or good enough. We want to change our self-image or social status. We want to be pleased with ourselves; to look in the mirror and to like what we see.

Ramana wants us to pause in this quest and ask ourselves, "Who is this unhappy person?"

All of our discontent arises from identifying our Self with the body or with thoughts that come and go, some with more frequency and regularity than others. All through these verses, Ramana has been directing our attention to the fact that we are not the body or the thoughts that come and go. We are the permanent witness of the body and mind: the changeless awareness that lights up every transient physical condition and malleable thought.

People who pursue "enlightenment" have usually reached the

realization that lasting happiness is not to be found in the world of objects. So, the quest for spiritual happiness is undertaken, following one's chosen regimen. And the quest is sustained by the hope that time and effort will cause the unhappy person to become the happy person. But Ramana wants us to recognize that it is our personal identity itself that is the problem.

Most spiritual disciplines are undertaken with the intention that the bound "I" should become liberated – a free "I." But it is the very notion of "I" that makes me bound. The bound "I" can never be the free "I," for it is tied to the body/mind. It is this identification that constitutes what is called bondage. So as long as we have the "I" thought, we will have the "I am bound" thought. We will be the unhappy person. "I" can never become enlightened.

There is a story in the East about a monkey who tries to steal some nuts from a jar. He reaches his hand into the jar, grabs the nuts, but can't get his hand out of the jar, for the fist now holding the nuts is too big to pass through the neck of the bottle. The owner sees the thieving monkey and begins to beat it with a stick. The monkey howls, but it won't let go of the nuts. Finally, the pain of the beating surpasses the desire for the nuts; the monkey opens his hand and escapes.

The "I" who wants to be free from bondage is much like the monkey who won't let go of the nuts. So long as the "I" thought is maintained, the ego "fist" will not fit through the neck of the bottle. No matter how assiduously we practice our spiritual discipline, so long as we are waiting for the "I" to be freed, we will remain as we are: the unhappy person. It is only by letting go of the "I" thought that we come to recognize that we are already and forever free and need do nothing to attain freedom. Bondage is not real.

If bondage were real, we also could do nothing to attain freedom, for reality is that which cannot be negated by time: it exists in past, present and future. If we accept bondage as our present reality, we have to abandon the hope that freedom will become our future reality. Reality does not change. Only the mind changes, but the mind is only a reflection of awareness and has no independent reality. It is a succession of thoughts illumined by me and falsely assumed to be me. But how can a fleeting thought be me? When the thought goes, I remain. Before the thought arrived, I was there. And this "I" never changes.

There is a famous verse in the *Amrita Bindu Upanishad*: "Mind alone is the cause for people's bondage and liberation. When attached to objects, it leads to bondage. When free from objects, it leads to liberation."

This wonderful clarity and simplicity is the heart of Vedanta. It is the heart Ramana spoke of as he began these verses in his prayer invocation. The chief object to which the mind is attached is the "I" thought. It is a compound of the Self and the not-Self: of the awareness that is me and a host of predicates that are mistaken to be me. When we inquire deeply and persistently into the question, "Who is bound?" we realize that no one is bound, for the "I" thought, the bound individual, is a fiction: a mental image superimposed on the ever-free Self.

Once this knowledge becomes firmly established, the mind loses its habit of identifying the Self with the body/mind. Thoughts continue to come and go, for such is the nature of thoughts, but there is no longer an "I" for them to latch onto. Freedom comes when the "I" goes; or rather, freedom is recognized when "I" thoughts no longer obscure the vision of truth – *Sat-Darshanam*.

Verse 40

Some scholars say that after liberation, form remains.
Others say that forms do not last. Yet others say, sometimes form remains
And sometimes it is lost. The loss of ego,
Which examines these three concepts, alone is true liberation.

Ramana concludes the teaching of *Sat-Darshanam* by addressing contending notions about the nature of liberation – *moksha*. We should be able, by this time, to anticipate how he will deal with the question: by asking, "Who wants to know?"

Some argue that so long as the body lasts, there can be no liberation, for the ego – the "I" thought – invariably accompanies the body. So, it is only after death that one can be free. Others argue that one can only attain liberation while in the body, for *moksha* is for the embodied mind. Others say that one can attain liberation both here and hereafter.

Without delving into particular points of argument, Ramana dismisses the entire controversy by pointing out that it is the ego who raises these questions, and when the ego disappears, the questions disappear.

Ramana is relentless. He will not let go of Self-inquiry at any point. And if we are to follow his instruction, we must become equally relentless. We cannot allow ourselves to be distracted by questions about the nature of the world, the nature of God, or even the nature of liberation. The ever-present question, the only question from which all other questions arise, is "Who am I?" Answer this question, and all questions are answered.

Such a relentless inquiry is needed because it is possible for us to explore the nature of the physical manifestation, its origin and meaning, without really abandoning our "I" thoughts. It is possible to explore the nature of God, and even to become ı devotee of a chosen deity, without abandoning our "I" thoughts. It is possible to do most anything and retain our ego. The only thing that will send the "I" thoughts packing is a direct investigation of their nature. Once they are found to be unreal – phantoms of the mind – the ego will dissolve.

And once the ego dissolves, once there is no longer an "I," there is no longer a "you" or a "that." Once we recognize that awareness is our nature and that it cannot be divided, then we realize we are unchanging and unlimited. Where then is the world? Where then is God? Awareness is all and there can be no second thing. The world and God only arise with the ego.

Meister Eckhart tried to express this truth within the context of Christianity by saying that the Creator arises with the creature; when we recognize our non-difference in the Godhead, creature and Creator dissolve into pure being. Eckhart's mystical realization never fit well within the dogmatic dualism of Catholic orthodoxy. Vedanta, however, is not constrained by dogma, and it has several teaching methods that can bring one to Self-knowledge without mysticism. Ramana bypasses many of the teaching methods used in the tradition to focus on one: inquiry into the "I" thought.

There is something very appealing in his method. After all, my major concern is me. When I come to confront my presumed identity with the body, I am seized by the fear of death. The Upanishads recount scenes of students asking teachers, in various ways, "Will I survive death?" We want to know if there is anything about us that will not be swept away by time. One certainty we all share is that we want to live and not die.

So, Ramana says, in effect, first things first: put aside all questions about cosmology and God and face the primal question: who am I? Who is it who wants to live and not die? And what hope can I have of surviving death if I am the body? Or if I am the succession of thoughts in the mind? None. Yet, there are the Upanishads that declare with confidence and boldness,

"Tat twam asi" – That thou art. How can I be that? How can I be the totality and not the limited creature I see myself to be? This is what the teaching unfolds. This is Vedanta.

When, through Self-inquiry, I come to recognize that all that exists is my own limitless awareness, Vedanta will have done its work. Then, I am free, even of Vedanta. This is what Ramana wants for us. This is why he left us this teaching. It may seem difficult, at times, but that is only because of our habitual ignorance and because we are trying to own the teaching; trying to make of it another "I" thought we can tack onto our résumé. When we let the teaching operate freely, without the interference of the ego, it will dissolve our sense of being an individual in a world of objects that we either covet or fear.

There is in this vision of the truth a capacity for love and tenderness that is overwhelming. It is not a state, that is, an experience such as we sometimes have in meditation or in a moment of spontaneous joy. It is a deep and abiding recognition that is available to us in all circumstances. It makes the unlovable, lovable; the ugly, beautiful. Self-inquiry does not produce the Self; it makes it lucid. We are always seeing it, but we are not always aware of what we are seeing. The phrase Sat-Darshanam does not mean revelation of a previously unknown truth, but the vision of what is.

There is a prayer in Latin called the doxology, or the "Glory Be." It offers praise to what was, what is and what will always be, in saecula saeculorum, which means "in the age of the ages," or "the time of the times." It is this stepping out of time while in time, this escape from being caught in the moment, like an insect in amber, that Self-inquiry offers us.

The beauty of Ramana was the beauty of a being who lived in this timelessness, from moment to moment. In his presence, people felt a joy, a sense of freedom unlike anything they had known. They had arrived at that intersection between time and eternity where the "I" thought dissolves. This was, by all accounts, an exquisite experience. But it was, nevertheless, an experience.

Ramana's legacy to us, however, is not an experience of the Self, but knowledge of the Self. Non-dual experiences have been had by many. They can be an impetus to Self-inquiry, but never a substitute for it. Earnest pilgrims who come to Tiruvannamalai and sit in the room where Ramana lived, hoping for some transformative experience, would do better to consult a competent teacher of Vedanta who can unfold the texts that Ramana left us.

This verse concludes the teaching. It ends where it began: by urging us to go to the source of the "I" thought, the Self, and to abide there in limitless freedom and love. The last two verses are written by Ramana's devotee who translated the Tamil verses into Sanskrit.

Verses 41–42

Maharshi Ramana has composed this pure work,
"Sat-Darshanam" in Tamil.
This sacred and uplifting scripture has been rendered into Sanskrit
By Vasista Ganapati Muni.

The Muni's words shine, reflecting,
As a wall does, the sweet and Divine voice of Ramana,
which gives the essence of truth easily
And is a delight for seekers of liberation.

One thing of importance might be noted in these concluding verses: Muni describes Ramana's voice as Divine. This may too easily be taken as hyperbolic praise; that is, as purely rhetorical in nature. It is important to understand that it is meant literally.

Ramana is not speaking as an individual. This is not his teaching. It may bear the imprint of his style, but the teaching is from the Upanishads. And this teaching is considered in Vedic culture to have come with the creation. It is from *Brahman* – the Self – and, therefore, not of individual authorship. This is not to deny human agency in the transmission and recording of the teaching; but it is to assert unequivocally that the teaching is timeless and, if the term be properly understood, Divine.

It is vital to realize this because we can otherwise misunderstand the nature of the teaching. This vision of the truth – *Sat-Darshanam* – cannot be arrived at unaided: it comes through the scripture and a teacher. It is not available through any other means. We cannot reason our way to it, although reason supports it. We cannot gain it through any experience, although experience does not contradict it. It cannot be produced by meditation or *samadhi*. If it were so produced, it would be dependent upon us and subject to time. So, when Muni refers to Ramana's "Divine voice" in this teaching, he means precisely that: Ramana is expressing the timeless truth of *Brahman* – the Self – the source and substance of all that is, the one without a second – Me.

The claim that Ramana speaks with a Divine voice should not be confused with the claims certain religions make about the inerrancy of their books and dogmas. The Upanishads do not set forth dogma, nor do they demand assent without investigation. It is a feature of the teaching tradition of Vedanta that lessons should be followed by a period during which students are given an opportunity to express their doubts and questions. Most every commentary in Vedanta contains *purva paksha* – objections and *siddhanta* – answers to those objections. Teachers and writers in this tradition encourage the student to explore all doubts. If any reservation about the truth of the teaching is not addressed, one's knowledge will not be firm – *nishta* – and ignorance will lay claim to the aspirant, using unresolved doubt as its grip.

Ramana, in these verses, offers us the vision of Vedanta. He may have been a great soul – a *mahatma* – and many may have had extraordinary experiences when in his presence, but if Ramana had only been another great yogi, his celebrity would be of limited duration and his usefulness to seekers of no lasting value. It is Ramana's situation in the *sampradaya* – the teaching tradition of Vedanta – that makes him a valuable resource for those who deeply desire to know the Self and who find their way to his verses.

Final Thought

When I came, at long last, to a serious study of Vedanta, *Sat-Darshanam* was the first text I read. I knew of Ramana and was familiar with the *satsang* literature that had been culled from his instructions to various people through the years. But the insights I was able to glean from these books were far from enough. I wanted a fuller teaching, so I turned to Ramana's verses, hoping to find it there. But the results were disappointing. I still lacked the key that would unlock their meaning.

Sat-Darshanam is not easy to understand. And many, I suspect, come to it as I did, without the requisite means of knowledge that alone can make it intelligible. The situation is exacerbated by some devotees of Ramana who post videos and write articles prescribing silent meditation on the question "Who am I?" as a sufficient means for Self-knowledge. But who is asking the question, and, perhaps more to the point, who is answering it? What criterion for truth is to be used in assessing the answers that may come?

Ignorance of the Self cannot be meditated away, nor will it yield to introspection, no matter how intense and prolonged. Ignorance will only yield to knowledge.

I hope the above commentary may be useful to those who have entered into Vedanta through the door that Ramana has opened. Many, I think, are attracted to the figure of the Hindu holy man that Ramana embodied in so classic a manner, but are unaware of the tradition he represents. If this brief work helps in some way to bring that tradition to light, it will have been justified.

This work began with a quotation from *David Copperfield*. Perhaps it is fitting to end it with a brief story from that novel, among whose memorable characters is a fisherman named Daniel who shelters the orphans and widows of his drowned comrades. One such child, Emily, he has raised as his own daughter. She has his heart. But that heart is broken when she is seduced and stolen away by a rogue. Daniel decides he will find his Emily and bring her back, no matter what it takes. It takes years. He travels to all the port cities and coastal towns in Europe. A man who loved less might have despaired and desisted. Not Daniel. Finally, he and his Emily are reunited. It is a tale of one-pointed devotion and heroic patience. And such is the tale of all who have come to recognize and abide in the Self.

It was not my intention in the introduction to this commentary to criticize the romanticism that draws many seekers to Ramana. There is in the ideal of the spiritual quest something noble, something necessary. Wanting to be the hero of one's own life is a fine thing. And those who have succeeded offer example and encouragement that can help to carry us through hard times.

But if we are to succeed in this quest, we have to know what is involved and steel ourselves to the task. Like Daniel, we have to be steadfast in our love and willing to persevere for as long as it takes to realize our desire – the very Self that is with us every step of the way, waiting to be recognized and embraced.

MANTRA
BOOKS

EASTERN RELIGION & PHILOSOPHY

We publish books on Eastern religions and philosophies. Books
that aim to inform and explore the various traditions that began in
the East and have migrated West.
If you have enjoyed this book, why not tell other readers by
posting a review on your preferred book site.

Recent bestsellers from MANTRA BOOKS are:

The Way Things Are
A Living Approach to Buddhism
Lama Ole Nydahl
An introduction to the teachings of the Buddha, and how to make
use of these teachings in everyday life.
Paperback: 978-1-84694-042-2 ebook: 978-1-78099-845-9

Back to the Truth
5000 Years of Advaita
Dennis Waite
A demystifying guide to Advaita for both those new to, and those
familiar with this ancient, non-dualist philosophy from India.
Paperback: 978-1-90504-761-1 ebook: 978-184694-624-0

Shinto: A celebration of Life
Aidan Rankin
Introducing a gentle but powerful spiritual pathway reconnecting
humanity with Great Nature and affirming all aspects of life.
Paperback: 978-1-84694-438-3 ebook: 978-1-84694-738-4

In the Light of Meditation
Mike George
A comprehensive introduction to the practice of meditation and
the spiritual principles behind it. A 10 lesson meditation pro-
gramme with CD and internet support.
Paperback: 978-1-90381-661-5

A Path of Joy
Popping into Freedom
Paramananda Ishaya
A simple and joyful path to spiritual enlightenment.
Paperback: 978-1-78279-323-6 ebook: 978-1-78279-322-9

The Less Dust the More Trust

Participating in The Shamatha Project, Meditation and Science

Adeline van Waning, MD PhD

The inside-story of a woman participating in frontline meditation research, exploring the interfaces of mind-practice, science and psychology.

Paperback: 978-1-78099-948-7 ebook: 978-1-78279-657-2

I Know How To Live, I Know How To Die

The Teachings of Dadi Janki: A warm, radical, and life-affirming view of who we are, where we come from, and what time is calling us to do

Neville Hodgkinson

Life and death are explored in the context of frontier science and deep soul awareness.

Paperback: 978-1-78535-013-9 ebook: 978-1-78535-014-6

Living Jainism

An Ethical Science

Aidan Rankin, Kanti V. Mardia

A radical new perspective on science rooted in intuitive awareness and deductive reasoning.

Paperback: 978-1-78099-912-8 ebook: 978-1-78099-911-1

Ordinary Women, Extraordinary Wisdom

The Feminine Face of Awakening

Rita Marie Robinson

A collection of intimate conversations with female spiritual teachers who live like ordinary women, but are engaged with their true natures.

Paperback: 978-1-84694-068-2 ebook: 978-1-78099-908-1

The Way of Nothing
Nothing in the Way
Paramananda Ishaya
A fresh and light-hearted exploration of the amazing reality of
nothingness.
Paperback: 978-1-78279-307-6 ebook: 978-1-78099-840-4

Readers of ebooks can buy or view any of these bestsellers by
clicking on the live link in the title. Most titles are published in
paperback and as an ebook. Paperbacks are available in traditional
bookshops. Both print and ebook formats are available online.

Find more titles and sign up to our readers' newsletter at
http://www.johnhuntpublishing.com/mind-body-spirit.
Follow us on Facebook at https://www.facebook.com/OBooks
and Twitter at https://twitter.com/obooks.